Selling Has Nothing To Do with Selling

Selling Has Nothing To Do with Selling

RICK FARRELL

iUniverse®

SELLING HAS NOTHING TO DO WITH SELLING

iUniverse books may be ordered through booksellers or by contacting:

iUniverse
1663 Liberty Drive
Bloomington, IN 47403
www.iuniverse.com
1-800-Authors (1-800-288-4677)

ISBN: 978-1-4917-5986-8 (sc)
ISBN: 978-1-4917-5987-5 (e)

Print information available on the last page.

iUniverse rev. date: 03/10/2015

Table of Contents

Introduction

This book is a labor of love of articles, white papers, musings, newsletters, blogs, and occasional rants. It allows you the flexibility to skip around and pick and choose what chapters most peek your interest. You will find the entire sales process covered with strategies and tactics from prospecting to closing.

The underlying theme is the information economy has neutralized the traditional value proposition of sales people. Sellers used to have a monopoly on information; obviously no longer. Sellers are struggling to remain relevant. Customers don't value their insight as they used to and this is resulting in challenges differentiating themselves from the competition, price pressure, breaking into new accounts, and simply getting a prospect to meet them.

In this book you will learn new ideas to sell in this environment. You will learn how to position your offering based on how you solve problems as opposed to how you provide solutions.

You will learn how to better qualify for opportunities and differentiate yourself from your competition based on your questions, not you self serving selling points. Know that if you don't change you will continue to be unique just like everyone else.

1

I Hate the Act of Traditional Selling
And Worse Yet, I'm Lousy at It

I do about forty speeches and sales training sessions a year. After every introduction by the moderator (which, by the way, I write in glowing terms), I always look around with this nagging question or notion in the back of my mind… Are they talking about me or someone else?

Because in the conventional sense, I truly hate the act of selling. Worse yet, I'm lousy at what we all call traditional selling. And trust me, I'm not exaggerating. I can, unfortunately, substantiate and validate this claim with examples of early disasters (read 'canned') in my selling career.

It was only when I came to the epiphany that selling has nothing to do with selling, that I was able to turn my career around and flourish. You see, I'm the epitome of someone who isn't a natural born salesperson. All my success can be attributed solely to learned skills. I'm a highly trained salesperson who relies on a disciplined sales methodology instead of natural instincts and talent to carry the day.

I learned that in order to sell effectively in the information economy I had to stop selling, pitching, presenting, answering objections, chasing and, God forbid, closing. I realized that selling, by its very nature, so often produces the exact opposite effect. The harder you sell, the harder it is to sell. Selling is repelling.

Because I wasn't one of the few and gifted 2%, I had to rely on a sales process that created trust, confidence and influence through my ability

1

to have a deep understanding of my customer's problems and business and allow my customer the freedom to self-discover their own answers and opinions independent of my selling agenda. Many salespeople today are being rudely awakened, like I was 15 years ago, to the reality that the tried and true skills of yesterday (personal charisma, persistence, hard work ethic, solid product knowledge and likability) are not enough to succeed in the information economy.

The reason for this is one word… Google. With two clicks, information is easily accessible and bountiful. The information economy has dramatically impacted the traditional role and value of a salesperson. In ancient times… the 80's and 90's… a salesperson's value was predicated on their ability to bring information, ideas and industry news to the table. That has been all but neutralized and marginalized by the Internet. So the remaining and sustainable value that salespeople possess to differentiate themselves from the competition is not to give information, but to **get** information.

Salespeople must build a business case for change, not a product case. They can no longer afford to be company-centric or product-centric. They now need to have situational fluency to understand the business drivers of their customer's business and help them identify and assess business problems, their consequences and understand the cost and impact of change. I call this the non-selling posture.

The reason I love the non-selling posture sales strategy is because it requires no natural talent or instincts. It is pure science and only becomes an art form when it is practiced at its highest level. The thing I hated about it the most was when I was learning it, it required me to relearn and reengineer everything I knew about selling. It required discipline and dedication to junk the tried and true old ideas and replace them with a practical, no nonsense approach that is pressure free and has a radical honesty with a willingness to walk away from opportunities that don't look right, smell right or feel right.

The non-selling posture takes a lot of the guesswork out of sales. What I always found frustrating in selling early in my career was that I successfully sold customers without really knowing really why, and I was outsold by the competition and I really didn't know why. My success rates were tenuous, random, unpredictable and not replicable.

Today I now approach every customer with the posture that I have nothing to prove, nothing to disprove, nothing to sell, no preconceived ideas and agenda, and no emotional investments in the outcome of the sale. This frees me up to take a position of neutrality and to build trust with my customer. This is where sales becomes fun and stress-free. Imagine going into a sales call with the heavy burden of proof being lifted; giving advice that is viewed with minimal suspicion; and selling without carrying the perception of having a conflict of interest.

So conventional selling as we know it today is dead in the water. However, I continue to see companies and salespeople being self-congratulatory at being very good at a game no longer being played.

They have perfected the ability to consistently hit the target, but it is the wrong target. The way customers buy, how they select suppliers, the time it takes them to make decisions, the way they assess value and how they create trust has changed dramatically over the last couple of years. However, the way salespeople sell would fit very well into a quaint Norman Rockwell painting; a lot of useless information, one-sided conversations, endless persistence, a firm handshake and a smile, lots of charm and personality and unending excitement and enthusiasm.

This just doesn't work anymore. Most companies are clinging and placing unwavering faith and trust in sales strategies that are obsolete, archaic and are designed to defeat them. This all results in lower margins, longer selling cycles, higher cost of sales and constant frustration and headaches for their salespeople.

I do find a fair number of companies that have seen the writing on the wall and have developed sound strategic selling strategies to meet the realities of the new marketplace. Unfortunately, their salespeople can't execute the strategy because they lack the proper beliefs and the disciplined tactics to execute them.

The following are some of the beliefs and strategies that fit very well into the realities of selling in the information economy and creating a non-selling posture.

- You are paid and rewarded for your questions, not your answers.
- To gain control you must give up control.

  Salespeople position their offerings for opportunity and customers are buying for the exact opposite motivation: fear and risk avoidance.

  Salespeople position their offerings rationally and logically and their customers are buying for irrational and illogical reasons.

- The salesperson with the best understanding of the customer's business will consistently outsell the salesperson with the best product, best technology and the best price.
- There are always two winners at the selling event: the salesperson who was awarded the deal and the salesperson who lost early and quickly with minimal exposure of time, resources and emotional investment.
- The best salesperson at the selling event is always the customer. Let them do all the presenting and selling.

  Don't tell customers how you can help them, how you are unique or why you are better. Simply tell them the problems you address and the problems you solve.

  Anyone can sell. It is more important to know when, where and under what circumstance to not sell.

- Persistence is the most overrated skill set in the information economy. Walking away from bad deals, unresponsive and uncooperative customers is the most underrated skill set in selling.

It's not what you sell; it is how you sell it that really matters.

Your value proposition is inherently valueless.

At the beginning of all my training sessions, I pose the questions, *"Who among you is a tad bored selling the same way you've been selling your entire career with very little change? Who's tired of saying the same thing every day and getting the same tired and trite responses from your customers day in and day out? Who is tired of having little control and predictable consistency? Who's tired of looking and sounding like every other salesperson? And who is tired of being in a job that isn't nearly as fun as it used to be?"* You can probably guess a lot of hands go up.

Most salespeople I meet are tired of traditional sales strategies that are designed to frustrate the hell out of them, put them at a severe disadvantage and leave them constantly guessing. And worse yet, they have no idea of what to do otherwise.

I have learned over the years that it is liberating, refreshing and extremely effective to approach every customer with the posture of 'let's get real': *"Let's assess your threshold for change. Both of us are very busy so let's not waste any of our time. Let's openly explore your problems and see if any are worth fixing. Let's have a frank discussion about your budget and authority to make decisions. Let's openly explore other viable alternatives. Let's make sure the timing is right and there aren't any competing projects that would supersede this one and let's do this one under the tenet that the burden of proof, information and selling will rest squarely on your shoulders."*

This type of exchange requires no innate natural ability. It does require training in most cases. Anyone can sell this way if they are willing to put aside their huge ego, put all the emphasis and focus on the customer, put aside all their information, forgo their emotional investment in the outcome of the sale, take off their selling hat and simply let the customer have the freedom to find their own answers independent of your own selling agenda. My belief is if I can do this, anyone can, since I have no real natural sales ability.

2

The Great Myths and Delusions in Selling

Since the profession of selling has always been considered in the past as more art than science, there have been a lot of half-baked, hokey and downright silly theories and strategies that have successfully infiltrated smart and well-intended sales professionals' techniques. Many of these strategies worked reasonably well in a bygone and quaint era where business was won on a smile and a firm handshake.

When presented with these myths and delusions, many salespeople grimace in disgust. Yet I consistently find that their actions subscribe to these dated, archaic and caveman-like sales strategies. However, in good conscience, I must disclose that if you violate one, many or all of these tenets, you can still enjoy success in your sales career. This is one of the true, sad tragedies in our profession. There are legions of salespeople who enjoy some measure of success, who perpetuate these myths and delusions. In my training classes, I call this madness "positive-negative reinforcement theory." You get just enough to get a modicum of success and never get enough to get what you really want. So the myths continue because you can be effective, but you rarely get to see the enormous downside in inefficiency because it is so masterfully masked.

The Myths and Delusions

1. <u>Winners never quit, quitters never win</u>. Actually, the most productive salespeople learn to quit early, fast and with minimal expenditure of resources and energy with prospects who ultimately will waste their time.

2. <u>ABC – Always be closing</u>. Closing is the most overrated skill set in selling. The most important skill set is opening. Too many salespeople try to close prospects that Moses couldn't close. Salespeople have been taught to ask questions that get their prospect used to saying *"yes"* so they can position their close with a final affirmation of "yes." This is insulting to prospects and they see right through it. The same goes for any facsimile of questions such as *"Can you see how this will help you?"*

3. <u>A great presentation will pave the way for many sales</u>. The presentation is the least important part of the selling event. The most important presentation at the selling event is the prospect presenting their problems, their consequences and their priorities.

4. <u>Sales is a numbers game.</u> This works to about $40,000 dollars in income. It's not the numbers, it's the quality of the engagement that carries the day.

5. <u>It is important to educate my prospect</u>. Actually, education too often is done prematurely without prospect input and perspective, and it too often leads to loss of leverage and control, sets one up for unfair comparison, raises unnecessary objections and reduces one to a commodity.

6. <u>An objection is a sign of interest and a request for more information</u>. This one is so silly and archaic, it doesn't even need to be addressed.

7. <u>Learn to love objections</u>. I've seen this in enough classic sales books; I had to throw it in for grins.

8. <u>Never take "no" for an answer.</u> The more inclined a salesperson is to hearing and accepting "no", the more inclined their prospect is to not flex their will.

9. <u>Sell the sizzle (FAB) – Features, advantages & benefits</u>. This style of selling that worked so well in the past no longer works like it used to. Companies pride themselves on their value add and value proposition, and from the prospect's position, their value proposition is valueless. What FAB works so hard to prevent, commoditization, it actually creates. The fatal flaw with FAB is that it puts all the emphasis on the least important person in the selling event... the salesperson. The only sizzle that one should sell is pain.

10. <u>Enthusiasm sells</u>. Ironically, enthusiastic selling kills more deals than it sells. The fatal flaw of enthusiastic selling is that one can't be problem focused and prospect focused and at the same time be positive, excited and enthusiastic. How can you ask thought-provoking questions that cover fear, risk, liabilities, potential loss. and at the same time be upbeat and enthusiastic. Of course you can't. It is totally out of context. How many physicians have you known who are upbeat, bubbly and excited when they are doing a diagnostic review with a sick patient? The other killjoy for enthusiastic selling is that one can't remain objective and emotionally detached from the sale and the outcome.

11. <u>Always answer your prospect's questions</u>. The problem with this tenet is prospects rarely ask the real question they are most concerned with. Salespeople fault by trying to be accommodating and courteous and they lose out in really learning what was the question behind the question.

12. <u>Find out what their needs are and you'll uncover their buying motives</u>. One problem here: people don't buy what they need. They buy what they want. Prospects don't buy drills. They buy holes. Too many sales organizations think they are in the drill business, when in reality they are in the hole business.

13. <u>Prospects buy rationally, logically and intellectually</u>. Most companies are positioning their offering in a well thought-out

logical manner, and their prospects are buying from their gut, their intuition and their emotions.

14. <u>First sell yourself, then your product and then your company</u>. Where is the prospect's situation and perspective in this equation?

15. <u>Everyone needs your product.</u> Nothing could be further from the truth. Even if they do need it, it doesn't mean they have the means, motivation, and authority to change.

16. <u>If you are a great conversationalist and have the gift of gab, you should be in sales.</u> How come we never hear what is most important: you are a great listener, you demonstrate empathy and understanding, you should be in sales.

17. <u>You are paid and rewarded to fix problems.</u> But not really. You really are paid and rewarded far more handsomely for identifying problems, helping prospects understand the cost of their problems, the consequences, and helping them understand the reality of changing.

18. <u>Pre-call planning is a must</u>. Too often, pre-call planning is a poor substitute for listening, questioning and coming to a meeting with no agenda to control or to sell. Pre-call planning is very effective when you are extremely knowledgeable about the prospect and their situation and you use that information to gain more information. Most salespeople use pre-call planning as a tool to control the agenda and the meeting and to steer the call in a direction that will get them to the conclusion they are seeking, instead of surrendering control and allowing the meeting to take its natural course based on the reality of the prospect's unique situation. Most pre-call planning doesn't factor in enough the consideration that no matter how pre-informed you are of the prospect's situation, you'll rarely, truly know the prospect's unique situation without getting their personal interpretation and rendition. Unless they're willing to admit to problems and

'fess up to their consequences, it doesn't matter what you know. You need to hear it straight from the horse's mouth. Unless your prospect is verbalizing their problems and are willing to emotionally go back in time to re-experience it, you don't have an engaged prospect.

19. <u>Internal sales training prepares salespeople to effectively sell</u>. Most internal, company produced sales training is simply marketing and product training. It convinces salespeople to regurgitate senseless product information without any perspective of the prospect's business and/or problems. It focuses all the attention on the least important party in the selling event. You guessed it... your company.

20. <u>Selling is an art</u>. True... for the 5% who are truly gifted. The remaining 95% of us mere mortals rely on the science of principles, formulas and processes to make up for pure natural intuition. If you believe selling is an art, *"it presents a self-fulfilling excuse for salespeople not to get better. If selling is an art, and I'm not an artist, then I'm off the hook,"* says John Holland.

21. <u>The customer is always right</u>. This assertion encourages salespeople to be approval seekers who rarely challenge in a professional manner the actions, beliefs and statements of prospects. Prospects frequently aren't right. The goal of salespeople is to learn when to professionally challenge and when to choose to fall back and exercise other options. Salespeople need to realize that they also project an arrogant air of always being right. As they temper their own assertions, they will find that prospects will tone down their own assertions – like attracts like.

22. <u>Salespeople should do what prospects tell them to do</u>. This is a close cousin to "the customer is always right." Salespeople have to diligently assess every request from prospects as to what

kind of return on investment they will get from their actions. Salespeople need to have the confidence to walk away from deals and opportunities that they deem a waste of time, energy, resources and information.

23. <u>Prospects are honest</u>. So often prospects aren't honest because salespeople paint them into a corner. Not only are prospects not always honest, but salespeople aren't honest always. How can you tell when a salesperson is lying... their lips are moving. When salespeople project a more neutral, unbiased and impartial approach, that is when prospects will return the favor and be more transparent themselves.

24. <u>The more thoroughly my prospect understands my value proposition, my technical information and my products and services, the more successful I will be in selling them</u>. The reality is, the more you understand their business and their unique circumstances, the more successful you will be.

25. <u>Price is the #1 criterion for purchasing for prospects</u>. All the research supports that out of the top five buying criteria, price is #4. When price becomes a driving factor, it is usually because of the way salespeople sell.

26. <u>Never ask a question you don't know the answer to</u>. This isn't a court of law. The whole idea is to ask questions to get your prospect's unique spin on it.

27. <u>Answer objections with feel, felt and found</u>. The problem with answering objections is so often you are answering the wrong objection. Rarely does the prospect state their real objection. The key is to ask questions when you get objections.

28. <u>Always ask open-ended questions to fully engage your prospects</u>. This is without a doubt the best questioning tactic. However, it only works when you have trust, cooperation and an open-minded prospect. This questioning tactic can be

especially ineffective in a cold solicitation call on the phone where resistance is high. When resistance is high, close-ended questions are more effective, since they require less time and commitment on the part of the other party.

29. <u>Show me a persistent, dogged salesperson and I'll show you a winner</u>. The problem with persistence is that it isn't highly targeted. There are legions of salespeople who are persistent with prospects who have no authority, no problems, no money and no inclination to change. The other problem with persistence is that it works only 50% of the time; salespeople don't know which is the 50% that works, so they are equally persistent with everyone. Persistence also doesn't work as well in the information economy because it is so hard to get hold of people because of voicemail, email, caller ID and electronic secretaries. I find persistence is too often a skill set overused to make up for poor selling strategies and skills. And as in dating, no one likes to do business with someone who is "needy".

30. <u>When closing, always position for a "yes" response</u>. The problem with this is when prospects are only given the choice of saying *"yes"* out of discomfort to tell you *"no,"* they will *"yes"* you to death. Prospects are far more sophisticated than we give them credit for. When you honor your prospects with the freedom to come to their own conclusions, independent of your selling agenda, you build trust and you save an untold amount of time not wasting your effort and resources on unqualified opportunities.

31. <u>Always establish early rapport with chitchat to connect to the prospect personally</u>. All the research that I see today, especially from the Brooks Group, underscores that prospects find that unsolicited, superficial chitchat with salespeople is distasteful and counterproductive (80% of respondents). So you better be sure you are with the right person under the right circumstances when you decide to engage them with light chitchat.

32. <u>Don't bring up price or money early in the sales cycle</u>. As soon as you've done your due diligence in understanding your prospect's problem, you should bring up your prospect's willingness to spend money to get rid of the problem. This should be done early in the sales process. Salespeople who wait to the end to have a frank discussion about price generally have a personal money weakness and they weaken their negotiating stance.

33. <u>Leaving voicemail while prospecting is productive</u>. Industry research shows that the average hit rate for leaving voicemail with prospects is 1 in 130. To underscore the futility of leaving voicemail, I tell my seminar participants that my best friends don't return my messages, how can you expect total strangers to return your messages.

34. <u>Prospects who want to "think it over" will eventually buy.</u> Unfortunately, prospects who want to think it over are saying in a nice way, *"I'm not interested."* The same is generally the case when they say, *"Send me some information, call me back next week or I still need to talk this over with my boss and I need some more time."* For some salespeople, these are still considered buying signals.

35. <u>Always be first in with your proposal</u>. This is especially not true in a very competitive marketplace. The general rule of thumb that will consistently give you a better return is, be first in to define the problem and set the parameters for the proposal and be last in for the solution.

36. <u>Don't ask too deep or too many questions because your prospect will resent the personal intrusion</u>. The salesperson who has the deepest understanding of the prospect's business will consistently outsell the salesperson with the best price and the best solution. Prospects only resent your questions when they don't trust you, or they have no interest in your offering.

37. <u>Always put your best foot forward: lead with benefits, don't bring up negatives, presume the close and have an attitude that the prospect should buy from you</u>. Since all of these fit a similar theme, I bunched them together:

   - <u>Lead with benefits</u> – Most salespeople are taught, especially when they are doing new business prospecting, to lead with benefits to establish credibility and interest. In the information economy, to establish credibility, don't tell them about how you can help them and what makes you unique; simply tell them the problems and pains you fix and address.

   - <u>Don't bring up negatives</u> – Bringing up negatives is how you create credibility and authenticity. If you never bring up negatives that you know the prospect is thinking about, you'll never be able to consistently get the prospect to share "the truth" with you. You'll also find prospects will give you the run-around and *"yes"* you to death, or give you long drawn out "no's."

   - <u>Presume the close</u> – The classic presumptive closes such as: *"Would you like to meet on Tuesday at 8:00 or Friday at 3:00?"; "Can you see how this can save you so much money?";* or, *"I'm assuming you'd be interested in learning?"* are early warning signals for prospects that they are dealing with a company-centric, self-centered amateur salesperson.

   - <u>Assume the prospect should buy from you and you can help them</u> – This tenet is probably one of the hardest, most deeply conditioned habits to break. When you take on the posture that you can help the prospect and they should buy from you right out of the gate, you tend to have a one-way, unengaged conversation with the prospect politely nodding, and never getting to the core of deeply understanding whether that prospect has a compelling reason to change or buy from you.

38. <u>Always have a positive mental attitude</u>. Many salespeople are into the cult of "Positive Thinking"; however, so often what they think about doesn't result in prosperity. This is an age-old problem. The reason is regardless of the surface level of positive thinking, we ultimately don't understand and value our true self-worth. If you really knew your true worth and were in touch with it, you wouldn't feel that something was missing. Arguably, positive thinking has surface benefits, but they are too often so superficial.

    You can't make negative thoughts go away by focusing on positive thoughts. For example, think positive thoughts for a moment... now think negative thoughts... now positive... now negative. For the next 20 seconds, think of anything other than pink giraffes. The problem is that you have to think of pink giraffes in order to remember not to think about it. Wow. Ironically, the more you try to control your thoughts, the less control you have. Sometimes the more you focus on positive thoughts, the more energy and power you give to your negative thoughts. A positive mental attitude is best characterized by not being emotionally attached to an end result. You maintain positive thinking when you accept your circumstances without resisting them.

    We compound our problems by giving them meaning. The act of being rejected only becomes a problem when we resist the rejection and try to change it and react to it. A positive mental attitude in the traditional sense tries to change our experience, and therefore compounds it.

    "It's all hocus-pocus. Stop chasing away negative thoughts and just be aware of them and accept them for what they are... random negative thoughts. All obsessions with scarcity thinking come from constantly reliving your past circumstances. If you didn't mind having negative thoughts, you would no longer have them. It is your resistance and your chasing away of thoughts

that make them so real and omnipresent. You guarantee their perpetuation," says Paul Ferrini. Positive thinking is too often negative thinking all dressed up. You can't force yourself to be positive and even if you do, it is just a surface projection and it's superficial.

"Experiencing your frustrations and rejections allows you to come to terms with them and ultimately release them. Denying and justifying our shortcomings with positive thinking without first truly emotionally experiencing them only represses them deeper to pop up at a later date. When you first see negative thoughts, don't judge or resist them. When you start to increase your awareness of them, you find that they don't have as much potency to run your life," says Paul Ferrini.

39. <u>Thoughtfully and carefully answer your prospect's objections.</u> I find it easier to get the prospect to answer their own objections because if you try to, you'll find that the objection they raised is rarely the real objection. How often have you found that you answer with perfect logic a prospect's objection, only to find they have an even more difficult one waiting in its wake?

40. <u>I really like people so I'd be good in sales.</u> Salespeople too often get into sales because they are very friendly, have lots of friends and contacts and believe these are winning attributes. I know far too many unsuccessful salespeople that you'd love to have as a neighbor, but you'd never want them on your sales team. They are very gracious, authentic and kind, and they end up being empty suits – goodwill ambassadors who can't sell.

3

Everybody and Nobody... The Decision Maker

It isn't unusual that by the time salespeople get as far along in the sales process to learn how decisions are made, who are the players who make those decision and what is the timing of the decision, that they are so excited to have made it this far that they quickly skim over it and rush to the exciting part, which is the presentation. Or, if they do happen to superficially inquire about the decision process, they generally default to the "who" question. The "who" question alone will generally get you the wrong information. If you ask the non-decision maker if they are the decision maker and they answer yes, what they really heard, or better yet what their ego heard was, *"Are you the decision maker to bring this to the final decision maker?"* The flip side is when you ask the real decision maker who the decision maker is, that individual, feeling pressure, palms you off on a fictitious committee that allegedly makes a group decision letting them off the hook.

Sometimes salespeople are reluctant to find out how decisions are made because they tend to be overly optimistic, lack objectivity and loathe doing anything that might ruin a perfectly rosy forecast.

The decision process usually includes a linked group of tasks, steps and a series of events with a timetable. Knowing the chain of command and chain of events is critical in timing your information. Once you understand the "cast of characters" you can now strategize your entry points within the organization. A general rule is to try to cover your bases by going broad and deep within a company when it is appropriate and always start at the top when possible.

Since prospects don't always have a well defined decision making process, you are going to have to map out your strategy in advance and share your own process with them. Keep in mind that the prospect will default to an information gathering process when they don't have a defined process. That leverages their time and always puts you at a severe disadvantage.

Salespeople too often don't have a firm grip on how long their selling cycle is and when it starts or finishes. They don't gather this information early on and they misallocate their leverage and control. *"Your sales cycle commences when your prospect shares an end date, a time frame or a serious intent. The time span of your initial contact, the time and the number of your meetings it takes to qualify your prospect and build trust does not factor into your formal sales cycle. The sales cycle begins when you start to have serious meetings and conversations about their requirements and your solutions and when it corresponds with a definitive timeline to make a final decision. The reason this is important to be aware of is because you now no longer confuse your sales cycle when you exchange information with the time you spend building trust,"* says Christine Gould.

Once you understand all the factors and variables involved in the change process from the initial contact, through the interest building stage to the steps necessary to the implementation of your solution, you can begin to effectively craft your sales strategy. Selling cycles are abbreviated when you go through a process of elimination of all the doubts, fears, insecurities, hurdles and delays that your prospect has to go through to make a final decision. Selling cycles and the decision process is locked down when you know the things that could happen positively and negatively with the implementation of your solution. As you become better acquainted with your prospect's culture, timing and philosophy, you have a better sense as to the practicality, convenience and reality of how your solution will be accepted and potentially implemented.

The following are some ideas on how to gain access to the elusive final decision maker:

- Don't fight gravity. Start at the top and if necessary, work your way down. Starting at the bottom of the food chain will inevitably stall your deals.
- Don't fall victim to the trap of selling and pursuing a prospect just because of their title even if they are the top dog.
- In today's environment, prospects that are buying value are located higher and higher up the food chain.
- The higher up the ladder one goes in an organization, the more the prospect wants to know what the salesperson knows about their industry, company and business.
- To get high in an organization, trade something they want for access. Ask tough operational questions that they don't have answers to so that you can get access to higher-level executives who can answer directly for you.

Here are some verbiage and scripts to locate the decision maker and better understand the decision process:

- *"Who needs to be brought into the loop on this?"*
- *"What is your process to issue a purchase order?"*
- *"If you became convinced that this service will achieve the results you need and you decide you want to move forward with a purchase, specifically what has to happen?"*
- *"What are the most important political considerations that I should know about in this process?"*
- *"Who or what are the potential wildcards that could veto this decision?"*
- *"When is the latest you'd like to make a decision? Why is that date important?"*

- *"There are two types of decision makers that I typically run into. 1) On their time, at their convenience, not a moment before; or 2) They don't have the time, predisposition or patience to drag things out. They are decisive and take the bull by its horns. Which one fits for you?"*
- *"So you can sign off on $30,000 yourself?"*
- *"95% of all companies I deal with have multiple layers for making a decision like this. Is your company like that?"*
- *"For what reasons would you choose to work with me and for what reasons would you choose not to work with me?"*
- *"In order for me to get the necessary resources to do a thorough proposal, I need to set up a meeting of both of our CEOs. Unfortunately, this is a company policy that I have no control over."*
- Negotiate for access. *"If I can set you up with an existing client where a demo can be given to you, would you in turn be willing to set up a meeting with your CEO, assuming the demo meets all your needs?"*

The following are very important elements to ascertain in the decision step:

- Who has the ear of senior management?
- Who can shoot your proposal down?
- Specifically who needs to be on board?
- Who are the financial stakeholders, champions, technical evaluators, cost evaluators and end users?
- What will you need to win support of others?
- Who signs the check?
- Does the CEO rubber-stamp this or are they intimately involved?
- What are the dotted line responsibilities of the individuals and departments that really pull weight?

If you are going to be an absentee salesperson at the final event. Here are questions you want to ask to increase your odds:

- *"When presenting to the committee, do you recommend one choice that you are backing or a couple of alternatives that don't matter one way or another to you?"*
- *"What is your hit rate when you go to the committee?"*
- *"What criteria will be important to them?"*
- *"What objections do you think they could possibly raise?"*

If you are locked out of the decision process and you believe your competition has the inside track, you may need to reevaluate your commitment. You always have the choice of backing out and not playing by their rules if they don't favor your cause. This decision will rest heavily on many variables including the health of your existing pipeline and how busy you are.

Once you have a prospect who has problems they can't live with, has the time and means to allocate to get rid of those problems, and they are in a position to make a decision to spend the money to get rid of their problems, then you have a qualified prospect. This prospect is now qualified for your time, your information, your company resources, your relationship and your self-esteem and passion that you'll now be putting into this deal. However, if they are not in a position to make a decision or you don't have the right access, then more than likely, you are just whistling in the wind. If you have really done your due diligence and properly qualified them for pain, investment and decision process, then I believe you have a certifiable, qualified prospect. They will definitely buy from someone. What we don't know for sure is who they will buy from. However, if you take the time and have the expertise to do the following I believe you will be very well positioned to be rewarded the deal:

- You helped them identify their problem in a way that they never thought of before hand, therefore differentiating yourself from your competition.
- You helped them do a cost/benefit analysis of their problem so they understand the costs of moving forward and the consequences of inaction.
- You took the position of a business strategist and built a business case, not a product-centric case.

Since you took the time to understand their problem better than your competition, it is perceived that you will now be in a better position to give the best solution. Remember the salesperson who does the best job of identifying and understanding their problems will consistently outsell the salesperson who has the best product or solution.

Since you did the preceding, you are in the best position to have the strongest relationship with your prospect and relationships are ultimately what prospects put their trust and confidence in.

4

An Inconvenient Truth: Most Salespeople Are Very Good at a Game No Longer Being Played

The world of selling has changed more in the last 10 years than any other time. The information economy has had a dramatic impact on changing the rules of selling and the strategies and tactics that it takes to be successful.

The following ironies, contrary views and thought-provoking ideas represent some of the new realities that sales organizations are facing in the information economy. The tried and true rules of selling have been negated due to the fact that prospects evaluate relationships, products and value much differently than they have in the past. Because prospects are more demanding and it is tougher for companies to differentiate themselves from the competition, it requires new beliefs, strategies and tactics for companies to succeed.

Problems

- All problems from your prospect are equal until proven otherwise. Don't go running off to the races to solve a prospect's problem until you've done your due diligence to understand whether that problem has consequences and is actionable.
- Even if you know in advance 100% of the problems of your prospect, you must allow them to verbalize their own version and rendition. If the salesperson has not taken the time to patiently let the prospect verbalize their issues, the salesperson won't gain the prospect's trust to solve it.

- All problems are universal. No matter what industry you are in, regardless of your product or service, all prospects change because of fear, insecurity and dissatisfaction.
- Since pleasure and opportunity represent a momentary problem-less state, even the pursuit of opportunity is an attempt to escape problems. All motives are driven by problems in some form or another, so always sell to your prospect's problems.
- Any problem, when fully discovered, defined and explored by a salesperson, contains its own answers, solutions, and course of action for your prospect. No problem can be properly resolved by your prospect until you help them find and address its causes from within.
- Prospects are more inclined to share information when you prompt them with questions that are designed to create or elicit hypothetical problems. Some prospects are more inclined to admit to imperfections before they will admit to problems. Effective salespeople will specifically detail all the positive things they know their prospect isn't experiencing, and let the prospect decide for themselves if they are willing to see and admit the large gap between perception and reality.
- If your prospects are unwilling to put the past behind them and they do not use the past as a bellwether for the future, you probably are not going to get them to admit to their problems.
- To establish credibility and interest in the information economy with prospects, don't tell them how you can help them, what makes you different or unique or why they should buy from you. Simply tell them the problems you fix and address.
- When the prospect has no problems, you have very little to sell.

Self-Esteem

- Salespeople proactively protect their self-esteem and rate of rejection by being very discriminating and discerning as to when and under what conditions they will make offerings. They avoid making premature offerings in situations where they have a high likelihood of losing.

- Salespeople put their self-esteem at risk when they are overly emotional about the outcome of the sale. This is why enthusiastic, positive selling has fatal flaws.
- Salespeople who take 100% responsibility for how they feel about themselves and how others treat them will greatly increase their ability to stay mentally tough.
- When boasting about your product's superiority or when putting all the focus of attention on your product, the only things that stand out are your own insecurity and irrelevance.

Listening

- Salespeople who struggle to be good listeners generally are spending too much time listening too intently to their own internal dialogue. Their focus is too much about their own needs.
- The art of listening is a selfless act when done properly. That's why it is so difficult for most salespeople.
- To be a good listener, one should be in the moment and always be aware of their prospect's situation. If you are not distracted by the coming attractions of an impending sale, or by lost opportunities in the past, then rarely will you miss what's important. What's important is what your prospect is thinking, feeling, and saying – this is the main event at hand.
- It isn't that salespeople are bad listeners; it is rather that they aren't good at asking compelling questions that will elicit answers that are worth listening to. Generally, when you ask compelling questions, you get compelling and revealing answers.
- The only time it is appropriate to be overly aggressive is when you are aggressively listening.
- Curiosity is the embryo of interest. The only time you really have your prospect's undivided attention is when you are listening.
- The first and most important sale in the selling event is to get your prospect comfortable in sharing important and potentially sensitive information.

Time Utilization

- The prospect you sell to and do business with will always pay in resources and time for those prospects you don't do business with.

- When you let your prospects make their own decisions independent of your own agenda, you free them of self-imposed limitations and they return the favor by making decisions much quicker. By operating this way, you save yourself and your company an enormous amount of time.

- Why do prospects not respect your salespeople's time? Because salespeople don't respect their own time and prospects return the favor.

- Salespeople chase, badger, over-inform, and they don't take the time to understand what is most important to the prospect.

- Time is the single most important asset salespeople have. They need to guard it and protect it and be very discriminating as to who qualifies for it.

- Time management is an oxymoron. You can't manage time, you can only prioritize it. However, salespeople too often organize and manage their time very effectively with prospects who don't have problems, budget, political clout, will, and decision authority. They get an "A" for organization and an "F" for effective time utilization.

- Salespeople should view their time as an inventory control system. The key characteristics of an effective inventory control system are time and money. The longer the inventory sits on the plant floor, the more it is going to cost you. Therefore, the goal is to turn and flip that inventory as quickly as possible. In the world of sales, what is a salesperson's inventory? It is their active pipeline of deals they are seeking closure on. If a salesperson viewed themselves as the CEO of their own enterprise, what would their goal be? To turn and flip their accounts as fast as possible, while at the same time keeping their prospects and themselves comfortable.

Closure

- Closing is a nonevent. The real event is opening. Opening is where 90% of all sales are won or lost.
- What is more valuable and realistic than closing, is seeking the truth. The truth will help you decide if closure is realistic.
- Too many salespeople are trying to close prospects Moses couldn't close.
- The more space and freedom you give your prospects the opportunity to say *"no,"* the less inclined they are to use it as a response.
- Seeking closure is a far more powerful closing tool than closing. The former is collaborative. The latter is manipulative.
- Closing infers being open to only one response... *"Yes."* Closure infers being open to the full range of possible responses. The goal of closure is to get prospects to make decisions.
- If salespeople aren't decisive about getting closure on their own decisions, they will tend to attract prospects who act in the same way. Like attracts like.

Qualifying/Disqualifying

- To qualify effectively, you must address the full reality of your prospect's situation. You need to know what are the competing initiatives; where would time be best spent based on the key priorities; where and who are the potential deal spoilers; does the prospect have the flexibility to roll out something new; are there the personnel to support it; is the timing right; and will the culture of the company be able to embrace and integrate the change? Once you understand all the variables necessary to consider changing, you can help lead your prospect in the direction that makes most sense for their priorities.
- Any salesperson can qualify an opportunity. The real pros are very good at disqualifying opportunities.
- Anyone can sell. However, it is more important to know who, when, where and under what circumstances not to sell.

- The salesperson with the best understanding of the prospect's problems will consistently outsell the salesperson with the best solution.
- One should be only as committed to sell as one's prospect is to change. If you aren't getting reciprocal effort in exchange for your own effort, it is a waste of your time.
- In any competitive sales situation, there are always two winners. The first winner is the salesperson who is awarded the deal. The second winner is the salesperson who lost quickly, effortlessly, and with minimal allotment of time, energy, and resources.
- Selling is just as much about being efficient as it about being effective.

Questions

- You are paid and rewarded for your questions, not your answers.
- The act of questioning, probing, and discovery is done more for the benefit of your prospect than for yourself.
- The best way to be heard, get attention, and make your case is to ask thought-provoking questions.
- When you ask stupid questions, you get stupid answers. Questions that are biased toward eliciting favorable and hopeful answers generally get inane, superficial and untruthful answers.
- Curiosity and inquisitiveness is to sales today as persuading, convincing, and cajoling was to sales in the past.
- Natural curiosity, being genuinely interested, and being inquisitive represent the new power of persuasion for the future.
- Asking *"What"* questions get you only a small piece of the equation, i.e., what are you looking for, what is important, what are your specifications and requirements, and what are your criteria for choosing a vendor? Instead, spend more time asking *"Why"* questions such as: why is that important to you, why do you want to consider changing now, and why would you consider switching from a supplier that you are happy with?

"What" questions tend to focus on what is important to the salesperson to get closer to the sale. Whereas, *"Why"* questions get to the real motivations and compelling reasons why prospects buy and what is at stake if they don't buy.

- The best salesperson at the selling event is the prospect. Let them first sell themselves and then sell you.
- In a sales call, what you don't know is ultimately more important than what you do know.
- Ask questions that are contrary to your best interests to build trust and to get to the truth.
- Good questions are posed more for the benefit of the prospect than the salesperson.

Selling Strategies

- What most salespeople think of as consultative selling is just a poor excuse for it. Usually, it is just transactional selling (a few safe questions) all dressed up with nowhere to go.
- All tangible products should be positioned and sold as intangibles. Products sold as a concept have a much better chance of upholding margins and building a strong foundation for strategic relationships.
- Salespeople should treat their very best clients as if they were prospects, because the longer you are with a client, the less you know about their critical success factors, since you are more focused on servicing, maintaining, growing and protecting, and not strategically learning about their ever-changing initiatives and priorities. When you are too close to the trees, you can't see the forest.
- Sales organizations need to cease being seduced by low-hanging fruit (quick and easy transactional deals) and seek first to build long-term business relationships that will position them as strategic partners. Once you get stuck in the role of a transactional supplier, it is very hard to move up the food chain.

- Most sales organizations are finding themselves in the inevitable position of being very good at a game no longer being played. Their sales strategies would fit very well into a charming and quaint Norman Rockwell painting.
- In real estate, it is location, location, location. In sales, it is timing, timing, timing. That means being at the right place, at the right time, with the right person, and under the right circumstances. However, most sales organizations operate and behave under the notion that sales is all about product, product, product.
- The harder you sell the harder it is to sell and find problems and a motive to change.
- Prospects don't so much resist change, rather they resist and resent being changed. Taking a non-selling change agent posture minimizes this hurdle.
- The best salesperson at the selling event is always the prospect. By allowing them to first sell themselves, they are far more willing to believe and act upon their own ideas. Few prospects resist their own ideas.
- Never answer objections. Get your prospect to answer them themselves.
- Your products and services are very unique and so is everyone else's.
- The most important presentation in the selling process is the prospects' presentation of their problem, factored in with the consequences, costs, urgency, actionability and timing.
- Your value proposition and value add is valueless.
- What you sell has very little to do with what prospects are buying.
- Selling's greatest allure is its greatest weakness.
- The prospect you do business with will always pay for those you don't do business with.
- The most important aspect of a sale is getting your prospect to share valuable information.
- Infinite patience in the sales process produces immediate results.

- Selling by its very nature so often produces the exact opposite effect. The harder you sell, the harder it is to sell.
- The best presentation is no presentation at all. Or, said in a different way, the best presentation is the presentation the prospect never saw.
- Great salespeople know when to quit and cut their losses. The odds are highly against you. Learn to lose quickly, early and with minimum exposure of time, resources, information and effort.
- Your success in selling will diminish in direct proportion to your emotional investment in making the sale.

5

Salespeople: Are They Their Own Worst Enemy?

If your satisfaction is dependent on certain results, then you are doomed to perpetual dissatisfaction. Whenever you want something so much that you make your satisfaction conditional upon receiving it, it is a sure sign that you are afraid to receive it. Keep in mind: if you were not afraid of it, it would be easy for you to receive it. One's inadequacy actually exacerbates it and that intensity actually scares prospects away. They sense that you are desperate. They fear manipulation and they withdraw. Often we unconsciously scare away what we seek. We must conclude that either we don't really want it or we are afraid to receive it. Both are probably true in most cases.

So don't try to always seek control. Often, we end up being controlled by the control we seek in our sales role. There is no greater feeling and emotion that will strengthen your self-esteem than the freedom and liberation of "nothing to lose".

Ironically, salespeople are forced to stay with poorly qualified prospects with low probability because they aren't strong enough to lose. Frequently, they are also in denial because as soon as they get rid of all their poor prospects, what activity does that free them up to do that they despise? You guessed it: new business development. This avoidance activity forces salespeople into a vicious cycle of acting like a gerbil on a treadmill that aimlessly goes nowhere. Being needy isn't an attractive quality to try to captivate and lure prospects with. We all experience this to some degree in our personal lives. Society looks at people who are needy as a sign of weakness.

When you expend all your energy and passion chasing phantom opportunities, you will have little left for when you pursue legitimate opportunities. When salespeople refuse to be taken advantage of, they naturally increase their own self-worth and self- esteem. Ultimately, confidence goes up and so does results. Keep in mind though; the real problem with your self-esteem is not really being taken advantage of by your prospects, as it is beating ourselves up because of it.

Lack of closure, resolution and getting people to make decisions is debilitating to one's self-concept. Salespeople need to first become good decision makers themselves before they can expect to get others to be decisive. The longer it takes one personally to make decisions, the more likely they will attract like-minded prospects.

Another contributing factor that eats away at one's self-esteem is when salespeople are constantly getting beaten up on price. Again, like attracts like, or, birds of a feather flock together. Salespeople who are skinflints and frugal will disproportionately attract price shoppers. Like anything in life, we unconsciously set ourselves up for failure because of our unconscious beliefs more so than the negative circumstances that we face. You can cure your problem of attracting price buyers only when you first decide to take personal responsibility for your own fate and not blame it on outside circumstances.

One can better manage their self-esteem and have greater control of the level of rejection they experience in selling by better coordinating their information. Salespeople set themselves up for failure by prematurely selling their products and services. Frequently, they are betting all their chips on losing hands. You can't be rejected unless you have made an offer. Protect your self-concept by being judicious with your information as to when and under what circumstances you will release it. Also be aware that you will allow rejection to negatively impact you because it offers you some measure of security and sense of control.

Many salespeople are into the cult of positive thinking; however, so often what they think about doesn't result in prosperity. This is an age-old problem. The reason is because, regardless of the surface level of positive thinking, we ultimately don't understand and value our true self-worth. If you really knew your true worth and were in touch with it, you wouldn't feel that something was missing. Arguably, positive thinking has surface benefits, but they are superficial.

You can't make negative thoughts go away by focusing on positive thoughts. For example, think positive thoughts for a moment... now think negative thoughts... now positive... now negative. For the next 20 seconds, think of anything other than pink giraffes. The problem is, you have to think of pink giraffes in order to remember not to think about it. Wow, ironically the more you try to control your thoughts, the less control you have. Sometimes the more you focus on positive thoughts, the more energy and power you give to your negative thoughts. A positive mental attitude is best characterized by not being emotionally attached to an end result. You maintain positive thinking when you accept your circumstances without resisting them.

Negative thoughts that pass through your mind are just a mirror of preexisting negative feelings that must be brought into a conscious level before they go away. They never ever go away when you suppress them or deny them. Denial is weakness masquerading as strength.

The other problem with positive thinking, excessive enthusiasm and fake cheer is that it is not real or authentic. Prospects see through your veneer and you can sometimes come across as a phony, stereotypical, superficial salesperson.

Enthusiastic selling and excessive positive thinking dilutes your judgment and your ability to objectively assess whether you and your prospect have a basis for a mutually acceptable reason for doing business together. Emotional involvement clouds your thinking.

Too often, positive thinking is a fake sense of security because positive mental thinking does not have sustainable lasting power. We now have plenty of burned out enthusiastic salespeople that it has become an occupational hazard. The best way to be positive is to not be emotionally vested in the outcome. And the easiest way to remain internally enthusiastic and confident is by increasing your probability of success by reducing your risk of failure.

The irony about self-esteem is that you need to feel good enough about yourself to know that ultimately you are unimportant in the selling event. You must have a very positive self-concept to be humble and to put your prospect center stage, with your product and yourself off to the side. Not being center stage for a lot of salespeople can become a tough pill to swallow.

So much of our day-to-day actions, activity and conversations are to confirm and validate our self-esteem. However, prospects only care and are concerned rightfully for themselves. So we have to be strong enough to place them first and confirm and validate their needs before our own. The reason this is important is because questioning and listening skills require you to temporarily cede control and require you not to be self-absorbed. It becomes very apparent that salespeople must have a very healthy self-concept if they are going to be able to take on a posture of "not knowing". The power of "not knowing" is a neutral position of looking at everything as new and fresh. Starting with a blank slate with every new client meeting, you are more curious and inquisitive. Also, you enhance your opportunity to be present and in the moment which always enhances rapport. By taking on a posture of "not knowing", you are more flexible and fluid and you won't be concerned as much about the outcome. It's liberating for you and your prospect. Moreover, as soon as you believe you don't know much, you are positioning yourself, ironically, to be learning a lot. When you don't know and think you do, you can't learn. This is worse than ignorance. Those who know everything know very little. In the beginners' minds, (not knowing), there are infinite possibilities. In the expert posture you are reduced to very few.

Another enhancer to self-esteem is your goals. Only three percent of adults have written goals. The key to goals is to be focused on the journey, not just the final destination. Over-reliance on the destination can have a reverse effect on your self- esteem. In sales, it is critical to emphasize activity over results. You can control activity, you can't control results. Have a plan of how many deals you want to make; how many people you want to talk to; how many appointments scheduled and attended; how many proposals submitted; and final orders received. By focusing on and monitoring activity, you will find yourself having days where you got poor end results as far as business, but you got lots of positive reinforcement from achieving the activity.

What can be even more powerful than goals is having a vision. A vision encompasses more than what you want to achieve but also how and why you want to achieve it. Generally, a strong vision will have greater traction and will be more sustainable than just having goals.

Self-esteem is critical in being able to constantly ascend the food chain of large accounts and higher-level executive contacts. Salespeople tend to associate with prospects whose self-esteem mirrors their own. The reason salespeople have reluctance to calling high in an organization or going out of their comfort zone and calling on marquis new accounts isn't because of poor tactics, but because of internal confidence. It's important to maintain your dignity and guard your self-esteem so there is a constant reservoir to draw upon.

Whatever isn't working in your sales position, you must take 100% responsibility. Once you do this, you will quickly learn that all frustration is solely with the past. What others have done to you or are doing to you that causes you discontent, is only an external version of what you are doing to yourself. When you stop beating yourself up, you will find that others will stop beating you up. Simply put, you bring into your sales life what you allow to come in. The problem is, we don't know what we really want or we don't trust it.

The key is to admit your mistakes, take responsibility, but don't be critical and be attached to the alleged corresponding negativity. The more you justify your failures, the more you hold on to them, the greater the likelihood you will project them onto your prospects and the greater the likelihood you will simply recycle them. Try to look at everything with utter neutrality. Most salespeople find themselves under a spell that as soon as rejection and frustration enter their minds, an experience will quickly come to confirm and validate that negative thought. That is how powerful your mind is. When you truly accept the truth about yourself and take personal responsibility for everything that you think about, you soon find out that all the random thoughts that come and go through your mind don't represent your true self. Your true self is peerless. You cannot put holes in it. It is bulletproof. You can only pretend to be frustrated or rejected.

When you take ownership and personal responsibility for your life, you position yourself to learn and grow from your mistakes. Taking ownership always empowers us. Denying responsibility will always disempower us.

The irony is, no one will beat you up or reject you more than yourself. There is no one who is as hard on us as we are on ourselves. We need to protect ourselves from ourselves. We are always our own worst critics. By preserving our self-esteem, we ultimately are kinder to ourselves.

It has been said that we decide what we want to see before we see it. We will find whatever we are looking for in our sales career because all perception is a choice and a matter of deciding to take or not take personal responsibility. So whatever you put your attention on, you become the creator of.

It is also human nature to milk our biographies for entertainment value, sympathy and self-righteousness. We love our scripts. Most of us would be nonentities without them. They are truly our false identity that we desperately cling to.

6

Building Loyal Relationships in a Disloyal World

Relationship selling is the bedrock for successful selling in the new millennium. However, most salespeople conduct themselves as if they were in a quaint Norman Rockwell painting, building relationships on a smile and a firm handshake, on friendship, on shared mutual interests, common background, charisma, personality and frequency of contact. This quaint, traditional and old school way of thinking is archaic and grossly ineffective.

Not enough sales organizations are questioning if this style of relationship selling works anymore. Prospects simply don't have the time, inclination, the patience or the freedom from accountability to create surface-level relationships anymore.

Did you ever meet a great glad-handing salesperson from the 70s and 80s? They had a winning and magnetic personality, a can-do personality, they were always upbeat and optimistic and they built friendly relationships instead of sincere business relationships. A psychologist would more than likely define their sales approach as self-absorbed, egocentric, narcissistic and center of the universe. The irony is that salespeople increasingly complain that their prospects are the same way. No wonder prospects sometimes act that way. Salespeople are so self-absorbed they don't let their prospects get their own needs met.

A recent movie, *"Good Company"*, perfectly typifies this type of personality seller. In one scene a rising star sales manager admonishes an aging and soon to be irrelevant Dennis Quaid about salespeople being dinosaurs if they don't change their skill sets. Dennis Quaid responds by saying that can't be all that bad since they ruled for millions of years. And the tragedy is, he's somewhat right. A personality seller can survive in certain sales situations and certainly in commodity sales, where being likeable will carry the day. Unfortunately, these positions are becoming more and more scarce in the global information economy where that type of salesperson brings little value to prospects. Sales managers are constantly reminded of this sales strategy when they are doing a pipeline review of their salesperson's prospects and the #1 criteria for a positive forecast is "they like me".

Personality sellers too often get caught in the vanity trap. They put too much emphasis on their own charm and persuasiveness. The focus is on them, not their prospect. And what do we know about prospects and who they rightfully only care about? You guessed it… themselves. Salespeople need to leave their magnetic charm in the reception room. Sellers who rely solely on their personality are limited to sell to others with similar personality traits and interests. True relationship sellers can connect to anyone because of the universal appeal of always putting the emphasis and focus on the other person. Personality sellers generally glorify themselves and their solutions and lack empathy and flexibility. They also seek to control the prospect. Relationship sellers let the prospect feel they are in control by empowering them to make informed and educated decisions independent of the salesperson's own agenda. They honor the prospect. Unwittingly, what personality sellers work so hard to prevent, they actually create. They are ultimately perceived as impersonal and uncaring and their strategy to appeal to prospects to like them is quickly becoming obsolete and irrelevant.

Too often salespeople are so intent on people liking them, they end up building meaningless long-term relationships with prospects who are at the wrong level, don't have authority and can't make "yes" decisions. Their need for approval and to get people to like them supersedes their desire to make a sale. What they don't realize is that one comes to harmony and connection with others not through approval or a need to please, but through authenticity. You build respect and long-term relationships when you have the courage to speak the truth and not sugarcoat everything. Prospects ultimately buy from you because they respect you. Personality sellers end up being the best player in a game that is no longer being played.

Don't fall in love with your prospect, fall in love with the process of learning their business and helping them understand their priorities and initiatives. You know you are too relationship-oriented to a fault when you are unwilling to let go of unqualified prospects with whom you have a great relationship. One question you should always be asking yourself is, if I invest in this relationship what will be my potential return? By the way, your prospects are constantly asking themselves the same question.

Many personality sellers claim they are relationship sellers when in fact they are just professional visitors, goodwill ambassadors and glorified order takers who bring no business substance to the relationship. They go only where they are welcomed and well received, eventually socializing on company time and dime.

Companies are now waking up to the fact that there is a deficit of true relationship sellers in the marketplace to recruit and hire. They are slowly coming to the realization that "the natural," who they sought out and hired in the past, can no longer bring the necessary prerequisite skills to successful selling in this demanding and challenging new marketplace. Too many sellers in the marketplace today are simply empty suits.

Relationship selling is a manner of building a business relationship on thought- provoking and incisive questions where the prospect formulates a belief and an understanding that you have the best solution without you even telling them what that solution is. Relationship selling is all about trust, confidence and understanding, and since so many products have reached quality parity you can no longer create trust like you could in the past with your product or service offering. You aren't selling features and benefits, your value or your superior product or service. You are really selling the advantage of doing business with you. Prospects are really buying your advice, counsel and expertise in their industry and understanding of their business and their problems. In true relationship selling, people don't buy from companies but from individuals. Trust shifts from product and company to the people who are selling.

Ironically, prospects will buy inferior products and service from salespeople they trust more often than they will buy superior products and services from salespeople they don't trust. Prospects don't have the time, patience or inclination to be an expert in every purchase they make. They rely on salespeople to demonstrate their expertise through their understanding of the prospect's business.

Because of a universal parity in products and services, the only remaining differentiation companies can rely on is their ability to engage their prospects in a unique fashion. Thus, trust is the #1 relationship skill in business. The first step in building a successful business relationship is through curiosity and rapt attention, which, by the way, is the highest and most sustainable form of flattery.

It's the journey that builds the relationship, not the end result. What you do from discovery to the close is what will determine the quality of your relationship. The sale is only the means to an end. The end is really the relationship you build and the opportunities it affords you in the future. Unfortunately, most salespeople, even with the best of intentions, are perceived as putting the sale first because of their egocentric approach.

Building a relationship on trust is easier said than done. For a lot of salespeople it doesn't come naturally. They may be likeable and friendly and knowledgeable but they might not have the innate ability to build trust and confidence with prospects who don't know them or who are guarded and defensive.

Learning your prospect's business allows you to create value. However, you don't create value with your product or services. Creating value and building a strong relationship requires you to be neutral and take a non-selling posture. Actual information is lost when we lose objectivity by emotionally responding (positively or negatively) about what we are hearing. By being in the moment we honor and empower our prospects.

As difficult as it may sound, we need to be empty of expectations. Building long-term relationships comes from first serving and then selling. Most salespeople mistakenly first sell and then try to serve and build trust through their deliverables. So often, they never get to the trust and serve part because the trust wasn't established initially.

Business relationship sellers are more concerned that people respect them and view them as a business resource as opposed to having someone like them. They ask tough questions, they are willing to walk away from relationships that no longer are mutually profitable. They take time to build relationships within an organization so they are never left high and dry when the inevitable day comes when their "inside guy" leaves. They also know when to have serious relationships and casual ones and they are always open to making adjustments. They are willing to be selective and discriminating to maximize their time and their returns. When it comes time to upsell existing relationships, they treat their customers as first-time prospects. They don't have preconceived assumptions, they don't take their relationships for granted and they patiently and methodically reestablish understanding of their prospects' new needs and objectives.

Effective relationship sellers seek to build relationships to get annuity business instead of short-term transactional business. Transactional selling is very expensive and raises your cost of sales. Relationship sellers always have their focus on long-term customer retention and development. Taking a long-term perspective, they are willing to make an investment in the relationship instead of just getting a quick hit or one night stand. Sustainable relationships happen when both parties view one another as equals. It is always more fulfilling and fruitful to establish relationships with prospects whom you trust and respect than with someone you don't respect, or you place too much emphasis solely on them and place them on a high pedestal.

Relationship selling, unlike personality selling, will ultimately be more fulfilling, will be more profitable long-term and will minimize sales burnout. By creating enriching experiences and connections through knowledge-based questions you will learn which relationships to pursue and which relationships to deemphasize.

7

Deal or No Deal: Minimize "Definite Maybes"

Unbeknownst to most salespeople is the idea that selling is all about getting prospects to make decisions, both small and large. Getting decisions that reach a conclusive "no" or "yes" and getting decisions that allow the prospects the freedom to decide "no," without the fear of a salesperson's full frontal counterattack. Therefore, selling isn't as much about persuasion and convincing as it is about self-discovery.

What sets up most stalls delays isn't salespeople's inability to close, but rather engaging prematurely prospects who aren't in a favorable position to make a change. Salespeople's misdirected desire to sell and provide solutions set themselves up to be used and have their time wasted by chasing phantom prospects.

To facilitate minimizing stalls, salespeople should take on a non-selling posture. This posture allows salespeople to be objective, impartial and allows their prospects to sell themselves as to whether it is in their best interest to change or not, regardless of the salesperson's personal agenda.

To understand why stalls are so widely tolerated and dealt with so poorly by salespeople, we must first understand the personal beliefs that salespeople unwittingly bring to their profession. These beliefs must be acknowledged and understood before salespeople can hope to change their behavior and improve their ability to deal with indecisive prospects.

- **Need For Approval**

    Too many salespeople enter sales to be liked and to make friends. By having a high need for approval salespeople aren't willing to ask the tough questions and call prospects on their stalling strategies. They avoid healthy confrontation because they put too much faith in the honesty of customers.

- **Buy Cycle**

    If you take alot of time to buy you will be predisposed to taking alot of time to sell. Like attracts like. This protracted way of selling and buying will naturally attract prospects who will stall and delay. The travesty is salespeople who are like this will have an overly-developed sense of buyer empathy and will be vulnerable to long selling cycles and the corresponding frustrations that come with it. If you aren't a decisive decision maker yourself, how can you expect other people to be?

    o **Taking Personal Responsibility**

    Salespeople who take personal responsibility tend to have shorter selling cycles because they don't make excuses and put the blame on the prospect for not making a decision. They take ownership, that ultimately they are responsible for deciding who to pursue and who to let go of.

Salespeople who also have long selling cycles and are vulnerable to stalls consistently don't manage these five key assets:

Time They squander their time on deals that they haven't properly qualified. They aren't discriminatory as to who they'll engage, and who they won't.

Information They don't judiciously guard their information. They freely and loosely give out their information early on, not realizing that they are losing their leverage and being reduced to free consultants

Resources They allow valuable company resources to be deployed without getting anything in return.

Relationships They act like goodwill ambassadors, indiscriminately building relationships with prospects who can't make decisions or don't have the influence to buy.

Self-esteem They set themselves up for failure by putting themselves in selling situations where they have a high likelihood of not succeeding without any regard as to how it will ultimately affect their confidence and long-term performance.

By squandering these five assets, they lose control and leverage and easily fall victim to prospects who mislead them, stall them, and abuse them.

The following tactics for stalls and put offs require a non-selling posture. These strategies are based more on getting your prospect to make a decision one way or another instead of forcing their hand and railroading them to agree to do something that eventually won't stick. These questions require finesse and a nurturing posture since they can be perceived as assertive in nature.

By honoring your prospect's independence to make decisions free of your agenda, you are making it easy for them to express the naked truth about their situation. This strategy can be used for closing deals or closing out deals, following up on appointments, locking down demos, presentations, or seminars, handling overly extended stalls, getting final approval from a decision maker or incessant requests for future call backs.

Since on average 70% of your sales efforts go to naught, than it makes sense to be just as good at closing deals as you are at closing out of deals. So much time is spent chasing losing causes. It is always very advantageous to get "no's" early and effortlessly without squandering undue time and effort. If you are discriminatory with whom you spend time with, under what circumstances, for how long and at what cost to your organization, you'll be able to maximize your assets. Also, by enhancing and perfecting your own personal buying habits to ones of low need for approval, short decisive buying cycle, emotional detachment and taking personal responsibility, you'll attract like-minded prospects who will be less inclined to use stalls and put-offs.

Generally, salespeople are reluctant to ask tough questions that put their offering at risk, and to get their prospect to share bad news. But, if you really want to be an advocate for your prospect, you need to give them every chance to disqualify themselves. Don't worry, that doesn't mean you instantly roll over. However, when you and your prospect don't waste each other's time, everyone comes out a winner.

The following questions strategically invite prospects to meet one half-way. Since these questions are "masters of the obvious," you need to present them in a nurturing way. Any way you can uses stories and metaphors to emotionally engage your prospects, the better. It helps them connect with the spirit of the message.

Generally, when your prospect wants to think things over, the only one who is thinking things over is the salesperson. The key is to empower your prospect to see the truth and reality of their situation. As long as you are engaging your prospect with thought-provoking questions and the prospect is answering them, you are getting closer to a resolution one way or another. By playing devil's advocate, you aren't afraid of putting a price on your prospect's procrastination. These questions are designed to flush out and contest the empty words and promises that prospects commonly dish out when you are getting stalled on a final decision.

The following are examples of handling stalls and delays:

- *"In the past when you've been forced into an awkward position where you've had to delay and postpone something, historically, do these matters revive themselves, or is it one of those things that if you haven't done it by now it will never happen?"*

- *"I'm willing to go the extra distance, invest my time and resources and follow this through if you are. But if you have too many irons in the fire and if you are ambivalent, then maybe we should drop it."*

- *"Mr. Prospect, I firmly believe when my prospect and I don't waste one another's time, everyone wins. Am I wasting your time here?"*

- *"Usually I find if it has dragged on this far it is the kiss of death. I don't want to be a killjoy, but I sense we've lost momentum on putting this deal to bed. What do you think?"*

- *"The road to hell is paved with great intentions. In relationship to this problem is it possible your grasp exceeds your reach?"*

- *"Can you level with me? You strike me as a straight shooter. We are facing the law of diminishing returns here. How realistic and viable is it that we'll do business together in a time frame we both can live with?"*

- *"You know if you put a frog into hot water, it will immediately jump out? But put it into cold water, and slowly turn up the temperature, the frog keeps adapting to increasing temperature until it adapts itself to death. I'm sensing our delay on this proposal is facing a similar fate."*

- *"It seems like the trail has gone cold here. Is that a fair assumption?"*

- *"Is this proposal a real hail mary and a shot in the dark or is the timing still on the money?"*

- *"You definitely have one leg in the icebox and one leg in the oven. What can we do to make it one way or another?"*

- *"I'm afraid if it hasn't happened by now, it never will. From your perspective, is this reviving or is this deal DOA?"*

o *"Before we drag this out further, and have me call you again next week, can we have a come to Jesus meeting now to see if this is still a good fit for you?"*

o *"Do you owe it to yourself or your company to consider this deal any further?"*

o *"Before we both jump to even more commitments to further follow up, which we both might regret, can we take a minute and be sure we are in sync about your interest and commitment?"*

o *"Would it be foolhardy and overly ambitious to say you are totally committed at this stage?"*

o *"Is this worth you sticking your neck out any further and prioritizing this initiative?"*

o *"I know you weren't planning to approve this until next month. Does it make sense to take the bull by the horns and resolve this now?"*

o *"What do we have to do to get you to make a decision on this one way or another so we can put this proposal to rest?"*

o *"I believe we have reached an impasse because of the classic saying, the devil you know is always better than the devil you don't know. It is always far easier to delay with something you know and have grown accustomed to no matter how bad it is than to risk the unknown regardless of the potential."*

o *"Is your interest active or inactive?"*

o *"I know even if a prospect may choose to delay or be forced to delay, deep down they don't like to procrastinate. The best thing to do is try to make a decision while everything is fresh in your mind. If you don't, as each day passes, you'll be less likely to make a decision. If I let you delay, I would be negligent in my job and do you a disservice. I'm too much of a professional to do that because I want to do what's right for you. That's why I'd like you to make a decision now, yes or no."*

o *"Let's recap why you originally chose to meet with us and consider us a possible partner, and find out whether or not it still makes sense for us to move forward. This way we can get some resolution on this matter one way or another."*

○ *"I'm getting mixed signals. I hear you loud and clear that you are still interested, but your lack of action speaks volumes. Am I to believe your words or your actions?"*

○ *"Let's draw a line in the sand, a drop-dead date. If nothing changes by that date, we'll consider it a dead issue."*

○ *"The million dollar question is, does your interest have any more traction?"*

○ *"How uncomfortable would you be if I asked you to make a decision today while the irons are hot?"*

○ *"What part of you wants to go forward and what part of you wants to cut your losses?"*

○ *"It sounds like you still have a healthy dose of skepticism."*

○ *"Even Congress doesn't take this long to make a decision."*

○ *"Is there anything we can do to entice you before you cool your heels? Waiting out the worst and hoping for the best isn't always the best strategy."*

○ *"I get the idea from your actions that your interest is fading and fleeting as we speak."*

○ *"Is your interest conditional and up in the air, or is it a slam dunk and a no brainer?"*

○ *"Usually when I give someone a proposal they really are in love with it or they have some questions or concerns. Which fits for you? It sounds like a "no." If it isn't a "no" and you don't have any questions of concerns, then it must be..."*

○ *"Usually when someone says they haven't gotten to it, what they somewhat mean is that they really aren't interested, but are uncomfortable telling me that."*

○ *"I can't convince you that you need this. If you really needed training, my guess is you would have already done something about this on your own. So we have to decide if this is worth going out on a limb to execute. You probably are wrestling with 'don't fix it if it isn't really broke'. Or, don't rock the boat on something that you can afford to hedge your bets on."*

○ *"What can we do to make this more than an idle, arbitrary curiosity? Otherwise, it will be easy for you to take the path of least resistance here."*

- *"You've been sitting on our proposal for a while. Does it make sense for us to think about sitting down again and wrapping up the details?"*
- *"What, if anything, can we do to upgrade and prioritize this deal so it isn't just one of those 2nd tier wish list projects? And if this isn't possible, do you have the stamina to continue down this path?"*
- *"I'm surprised you haven't made a decision on this. You strike me as a take-charge decisive person."*
- *"You aren't going to have me believe you are going to be indecisive and draw this decision out, are you?"*
- *"Let me play devil's advocate. You probably haven't made a decision on this for a good reason. Is that reason at all related to this no longer being a priority for you? Then what is it?"*
- *"I get the sense that you are dangerously getting to that point that you can easily write this off as an idea past its prime."*
- *"I'm doing some forecasting on this account with corporate. They want me to find out from you realistically as to where you stand, for better or for worse. So where do you stand?"*
- *"I'm afraid that the longer we draw this out the more these problems get factored into the cost of doing business and are looked upon as something that just comes with the territory and nothing will change because of that."*
- *"Has this fallen off your radar screen?"*
- *"Have I grossly overestimated your interest and commitment and if I have, may I apologize?"*
- *"As I see it, I have two choices here. I can be real patient and persistent, or we can jointly decide now one way or another as to whether we proceed. Which do you prefer?"*
- *"Sometimes clients lack resolve, commitment and conviction to move forward. In principle, they are sold, but in respect to practicality, it is too inconvenient and not high enough on their radar screen to take action."*
- *"Does it disappoint you or surprise you that you haven't made a decision on this as of yet?"*

- *"When you've had something in the past that was important to make a decision about, what was your sense of urgency? What's different now?"*

- *"I must, like you, spend my time very judiciously and productively. Please don't spare my feelings by telling me what you think I want to hear."*

- *"What can we do to pull the trigger or pull the plug?"*

- *"The biggest challenge I face is customers have a genuine and sincere interest to change, but for a variety of reasons have a passive, casual and idle interest to do anything about it. Does this describe your quandary?"*

- *"I get the sense that there is a little part of you that says if it hasn't happened by now, it unfortunately will never happen."*

- *"Is this something you have to think long and hard about or is this pretty straightforward?"*

- *"Are you afraid haste will make waste?"*

- *"What I want to try to avoid is going through the motions of making a decision two months from now that could have just as easily been done two months earlier."*

- *"Are there any advantages from your perspective to doing this sooner rather than later?"*

- *"Is this a problem that has run its course? You seem not to be under the gun to fix it. Do you now have bigger fish to fry?"*

- *"Have we reached a point of diminishing returns here?"*

- *"You strike me as a take charge-person, the kind who takes the bull by its horns. Can we make a decision today?"*

- *"You aren't 100% sold on moving forward, are you?"*

- *"From your perspective, what would you have to gain or to lose by not moving ahead with this?"*

- *"So that I can follow up with you in the most professional manner and not be a stereotypical salesperson who is going to waste your time and be a pest, is your interest passive and casual or is it genuine and actionable?"*

- *"If you were a betting man, would you say this deal is getting ready to close or implode?"*

o   *"I get the sense we've been in a holding pattern on this proposal because I'm pushing you to do something that isn't in your best interests or the timing isn't optimal for you."*

o   *"You are dangerously in that grey zone where you are getting just enough to be comfortable but you aren't getting enough to be very content. Are you willing to back up your intentions with action?"*

o   *"Let's say you had to make a decision today. If I put a gun to my head and told you which will it be, yea or nay, what would your answer be?"*

o   *"What exactly did you want to think over?"*

o   *"What are you going to think about? What more do you need? Then it sounds like you've made up your mind."*

o   *"If your schedule hasn't permitted you to commit to taking 10 minutes to review this with your boss, then what does that tell you about your problem?"*

o   *"You are between a rock and a hard place. At this stage which is more important: the problem at hand and the fact that it is costing you $1 million a year, or the problem of finding time to decide on this?"*

o   *"It sounds like you are in a position to make a commitment only under ideal and optimal conditions and since you don't have that luxury now, should we pursue this any more with you?"*

o   *"I want to apologize. We are at a standstill here. I might have grossly misjudged your intentions. Here I'm trying to get closure and you aren't even sure if you are really interested anymore. Where do we stand?"*

o   *"When something is relatively unimportant and not a high priority for you, how do you usually dispense with it? Is that any different from our situation?"*

o   *"My guess is that we will continue to have this conversation until the pain of change is less than the pain of the status quo. You can afford to drag your feet on this because for the time being, you have a high threshold for your problem based on your other priorities."*

- ○ *"My experience tells me that people rarely want more of what they already have in abundance. Since business is very good for you now, I could see where you don't have a compelling reason to act now."*

- ○ *"I'm not so naïve as to recognize that a satisfied need is rarely a motivation. If for example, you go to your favorite French restaurant and have a wonderful 4-course meal, and you are totally full and satisfied and they bring you your favorite soufflé dessert, you will turn them down because you are full and satisfied. I get the sense you are in a similar situation."*

- ○ *"You have not yet overcome or reconciled the 'twin evil forces' of change, which are time and habit. You are in the classic dead man's zone. You are getting just enough to make it worthwhile but not enough to really get what you want. I believe that is why we are at an impasse or standstill on this proposal."*

- ○ *"It sounds like you are overextended, overcommitted and stretched too thin. So does it make sense for me to commit my time to follow up with you?"*

- ○ *"Sounds like you want to commit, but you aren't sure what you are committing to."*

- ○ *"Based on my many years in the business, can I tell you what has happened many times in the past? It might not be relevant here. When I call you back in 10 days and your secretary tells you that I am on the line, that is when you'll make a decision. If this is the case, can w possibly accelerate this process?"*

- ○ *"Are you willing to go out on a limb, grab the bull by the horns and expedite this?"*

- ○ *"I am afraid the longer I drag this out with you, that it will become a problem past its prime."*

- ○ *"I always feel a little awkward and embarrassed to ask this, but I feel I must ask in all fairness to you. One of my greatest fears is that I railroaded you into agreeing to consider us without giving you the chance to do otherwise. Did I force your hand in this?"*

- ○ *"Let me throw caution to the wind and possibly shoot myself in the foot. I know your time is very precious but if you truly believed in your gut that we could help you, you would have*

*already made a decision. And the fact that you haven't tells me
that maybe this decision is possibly past its prime."*

o *"I get the sense your interest is chilling and is possibly going
into a deep freeze. Is this a cold lead now?"*

o *"Wouldn't it be safe to characterize your interest as no longer
being hot to trot?"*

o *"I think we've hit a brick wall. So that I can adjust my follow-up
with you appropriately, how timely or untimely is this for you?"*

o *"Just so we both understand one another. This isn't my hobby,
although I love it and can't think of doing anything else. This
is how I clothe, feed, and support my family. So it is critical I
respect your time as much as mine. If you aren't convinced this
is right for you, I would greatly appreciate you telling me so.
That way I won't waste either of our precious time."*

o *"On your to-do list, where does this fit? My intention isn't to
push, but we've met quite a few times and I have followed up
with you diligently many times. It seems we aren't getting any
closer to getting a resolution. Can I ask, is there a decision on
this in our future?"*

o *"I know you want to think it over some and get all your ducks
in a row, and I think you should. I don't want to take that away
from you. Sometimes I can help my prospects by asking them
some questions that will lead them to realize that this isn't a
good decision, or to firm up and strengthen their conviction that
this is the right decision. Let's take a few moments to review the
pros and cons of moving forward and maybe it can help us get
a decision."*

o *"We have potentially a classic conflict of interest here. You
have problems but don't have the time to give them top priority.
Unfortunately, the status quo usually prevails in these cases.
Unless you are the exception to the rule, your delay fondly
reminds me of my bachelor days when I had leftover food in
my refrigerator and it wasn't bad enough to throw out but it
wasn't appealing enough to eat. And I finally took action when
my fiancée threatened to throw me out. I get the sense you are
facing a similar quandary."*

Hope springs eternal in the peddler's heart. Ask questions that get the truth, instead of just getting a glimmer of hope. Don't be afraid to ask questions that could render your "sales cause" hopeless. Don't be deluded into thinking that if you don't bring up something negative, they won't bring it up on their own or won't think about it. And, if they aren't willing to make a decision and you think you are at a point of no return, don't hesitate to force the issue and accept the inevitable "no". This strategy clearly has its risks, yet so does the long drawn-out patient route that obviously leads nowhere.

8

The Death of Product Pitching

Most companies and their salespeople covet their value add, their features and benefits, and their value proposition as if it were the Holy Grail. The reality is all value propositions are inherently valueless. The feature and benefit style of selling that has served companies so well in the past no longer works. It is tried, but no longer true.

Firms that have successfully relied on this kind of selling to differentiate themselves from their competition, translate their value, maintain their margins and avoid the dreaded price focus are discovering that this once-dependable method is backfiring. The irony is that in today's highly competitive marketplace, where information runs freely, companies actually create the commoditization they work so hard to avoid.

Value added selling is rooted in old economic conditions using time-honored traditions, a sales strategy from another era entirely, some unimaginable distant epoch of 5-10 years ago. This artificial style of selling that, until recently, has withstood the test of time, only homogenizes your offering. Value proposition selling is just roll-the-dice selling, where you are on autopilot and you cross your fingers and show up and throw up. It is driven by the love to talk and the fear to listen. It is jargon on crack.

Salespeople operate under the quaint notion that it is their God-given right to sell their features and benefits. Since it states in the Sales Constitution that all products are not created equal, it is your solemn right and salesman duty to show prospects the correct way to the Promised Land. However, no one has the corner on absolute truth.

If it was all this easy and it really was all about our product's capabilities and market leadership, we would all be retired now because the product would speak for itself and sell itself. Actually, we would all be out of a job and a profession if it were all about the product. If it were, they certainly would not need most salespeople.

In today's marketplace, the feature and benefit sales methodology that so many companies use to differentiate themselves actually makes them look and sound like everyone else, completely marginalizing their value proposition. The sales reps all sing from the same hymnbook and they all reduce themselves unwittingly to the lowest common denominator. What a lot of sales reps don't realize, however, is that many customers work very hard to set reps up to sell this way.

Illustrating this point, I once gave a presentation at a company where a buyer attending the meeting pulled me aside and proceeded to explain this exact strategy and how it benefited him by getting all the suppliers to believe they weren't different at all. As soon as the reps were convinced they were basically interchangeable, he noted, they would all reduce their pricing.

The irony is all companies, big or small, sophisticated or unworldly, in all industries, covering all products and all services, intangibles or tangibles, sell the same way. They sanitize and whitewash their offering by using common standards, open architecture specifications that multiple vendors can easily meet. In the end, it becomes a wash. The very thing that feature and benefit selling tries to protect against, it reinforces. Their self-indulgent presentations reflect mostly minimum standards and lowest common denominators for being considered or just staying in business. It is truly a zero-sum game. Companies are just grounding down one another to a lackluster sameness.

In respect to your features and benefits, there is ample anecdotal research that prospects perceive differences between competing products and services to be considerably less measurable and important than salespeople think it is. On an average sales call, a salesperson touts

6 to 8 features and the average prospect can only remember one product feature and frequently that was inaccurately recalled.

That correlates well with industry accepted research that says the success of a salesperson is based only on 10% product and technical expertise, 15% on selling skills, 25% on relationship and people skills, and 50% on beliefs and attitude (goals, motivation, and beliefs about sales).

A recent study by the National Association of Manufacturers found that there is a superfluous 30% added value on products that are valueless. Vendors are supplying products and services that customers do not want, need, or recognize. Our hype and over-reliance on featuring our products' attributes cause this. We use our products as a stick to try to beat people into submission. The harder you attack and hold onto your products' features and benefits, the harder you hold onto the belief that it is universally right for everyone. It is a vicious cycle.

The irony is that prospects will do everything possible to have you sell your features and benefits, outline your solutions, have you ask as few questions as possible to learn more about them, and make premature recommendations, when the exact opposite is what they desperately need and want. Be aware that they will deny you an authentic, professional approach because of fear and apprehension of full disclosure. That is why you get blank stares and restlessness from prospects after you have expertly showed them how you can help them, and you ultimately walk away with nothing to show for your efforts. There is an old fable that captures this concept well: the mythical story of Samson slaying 10,000 Philistines with the jawbone of an ass. Salespeople are doing the same thing daily by killing sales opportunities with the same weapon. When prospects ask if you can help them, inquire about what makes you better, ask for a proposal, request your pricing… what they really are asking and what they really care about is, *"Do you understand me?"*

Value based (features and benefit) selling does not work as well today because prospects are more savvy and sophisticated. They have less time to be influenced with all your information (especially as you move up the food chain), they are held more accountable in their purchasing decisions, and the information you have can be ascertained and accessed through alternative channels.

In the knowledge based economy, the value of a salesperson is judged not on what they know about their product but on what they can learn about their prospects' problems and critical success factors. Unlike in the Dark Ages, leading with your product information and solutions now is looked upon with suspicion.

In the Internet era, sales organizations can no longer get away with placing pathetic faith and stock in their products and solutions. We eulogize and romanticize our products and service offerings as if they were the end all, the real thing. We can no longer afford to treat prospects as Pavlovian dogs that are shaped by only one stimulus—our features and benefits. All products and services are intrinsically valueless. We need to put more faith and value into our prospect's problems, their corresponding consequences, and learning the intricacies of their business so we can build a business case that supports change or recognizes that change is not feasible.

By playing the role of a product pitchman and being a talking brochure, we end up simply parroting what our competition is doing: advancing our position negligibly. By being exactly like all the other competitors, we naively participate in the parade of venders who are like the lemmings, blindly and without question, marching to the sea to their inevitable demise.

Like professional boxers, you cannot just be equal to the incumbent to be a challenger; you must be demonstrably better. Too often, salespeople are forcing their will and agenda on prospects before they have firmly established if their prospect has a compelling and driving reason to change. You cannot sell value until your prospect has voiced what value looks like to them.

Prospects do not buy in a vacuum where there are no other variables or priorities to consider, yet salespeople conduct themselves as if they did. Roughly 60% of all sales are lost to a "no buy" or "no change". Selling your value proposition does not account for the prospects who do not buy from anyone. Salespeople waste untold amounts of time and credibility establishing product superiority with a prospect who has not firmly decided they are truly committed to changing. They are trying to close someone Moses or the Prophet Mohammed could not close.

Most companies and their salespeople covet their value add, their features and benefits, and their value proposition as if it were the Holy Grail. The reality is all value propositions are inherently valueless. The feature and benefit style of selling that has served companies so well in the past no longer works. It is tried, but no longer true.

Firms that have successfully relied on this kind of selling to differentiate themselves from their competition, translate their value, maintain their margins and avoid the dreaded price focus are discovering that this once-dependable method is backfiring. The irony is that in today's highly competitive marketplace, where information runs freely, companies actually create the commoditization they work so hard to avoid.

Value added selling is rooted in old economic conditions using time-honored traditions, a sales strategy from another era entirely, some unimaginable distant epoch of 5-10 years ago. This artificial style of selling that, until recently, has withstood the test of time, only homogenizes your offering. Value proposition selling is just roll-the-dice selling, where you are on autopilot and you cross your fingers and show up and throw up. It is driven by the love to talk and the fear to listen. It is jargon on crack.

Salespeople operate under the quaint notion that it is their God-given right to sell their features and benefits. Since it states in the Sales Constitution that all products are not created equal, it is your solemn right and salesman duty to show prospects the correct way to the Promised Land. However, no one has the corner on absolute truth.

If it was all this easy and it really was all about our product's capabilities and market leadership, we would all be retired now because the product would speak for itself and sell itself. Actually, we would all be out of a job and a profession if it were all about the product. If it were, they certainly would not need most salespeople.

In today's marketplace, the feature and benefit sales methodology that so many companies use to differentiate themselves actually makes them look and sound like everyone else, completely marginalizing their value proposition. The sales reps all sing from the same hymnbook and they all reduce themselves unwittingly to the lowest common denominator. What a lot of sales reps don't realize, however, is that many customers work very hard to set reps up to sell this way.

Illustrating this point, I once gave a presentation at a company where a buyer attending the meeting pulled me aside and proceeded to explain this exact strategy and how it benefited him by getting all the suppliers to believe they weren't different at all. As soon as the reps were convinced they were basically interchangeable, he noted, they would all reduce their pricing.

The irony is all companies, big or small, sophisticated or unworldly, in all industries, covering all products and all services, intangibles or tangibles, sell the same way. They sanitize and whitewash their offering by using common standards, open architecture specifications that multiple vendors can easily meet. In the end, it becomes a wash. The very thing that feature and benefit selling tries to protect against, it reinforces. Their self-indulgent presentations reflect mostly minimum standards and lowest common denominators for being considered or just staying in business. It is truly a zero-sum game. Companies are just grounding down one another to a lackluster sameness.

In respect to your features and benefits, there is ample anecdotal research that prospects perceive differences between competing products and services to be considerably less measurable and important than salespeople think it is. On an average sales call, a salesperson touts 6 to 8 features and the average prospect can only remember one product feature and frequently that was inaccurately recalled.

That correlates well with industry accepted research that says the success of a salesperson is based only on 10% product and technical expertise, 15% on selling skills, 25% on relationship and people skills, and 50% on beliefs and attitude (goals, motivation, and beliefs about sales).

A recent study by the National Association of Manufacturers found that there is a superfluous 30% added value on products that are valueless. Vendors are supplying products and services that customers do not want, need, or recognize. Our hype and over-reliance on featuring our products' attributes cause this. We use our products as a stick to try to beat people into submission. The harder you attack and hold onto your products' features and benefits, the harder you hold onto the belief that it is universally right for everyone. It is a vicious cycle.

The irony is that prospects will do everything possible to have you sell your features and benefits, outline your solutions, have you ask as few questions as possible to learn more about them, and make premature recommendations, when the exact opposite is what they desperately need and want. Be aware that they will deny you an authentic, professional approach because of fear and apprehension of full disclosure. That is why you get blank stares and restlessness from prospects after you have expertly showed them how you can help them, and you ultimately walk away with nothing to show for your efforts. There is an old fable that captures this concept well: the mythical story of Samson slaying 10,000 Philistines with the jawbone of an ass. Salespeople are doing the same thing daily by killing sales opportunities with the same weapon. When prospects ask if you can help them, inquire about what makes you better, ask for a proposal, request your pricing… what they really are asking and what they really care about is, *"Do you understand me?"*

Value based (features and benefit) selling does not work as well today because prospects are more savvy and sophisticated. They have less time to be influenced with all your information (especially as you move up the food chain), they are held more accountable in their purchasing decisions, and the information you have can be ascertained and accessed through alternative channels.

In the knowledge based economy, the value of a salesperson is judged not on what they know about their product but on what they can learn about their prospects' problems and critical success factors. Unlike in the Dark Ages, leading with your product information and solutions now is looked upon with suspicion.

In the Internet era, sales organizations can no longer get away with placing pathetic faith and stock in their products and solutions. We eulogize and romanticize our products and service offerings as if they were the end all, the real thing. We can no longer afford to treat prospects as Pavlovian dogs that are shaped by only one stimulus—our features and benefits. All products and services are intrinsically valueless. We need to put more faith and value into our prospect's problems, their corresponding consequences, and learning the intricacies of their business so we can build a business case that supports change or recognizes that change is not feasible.

By playing the role of a product pitchman and being a talking brochure, we end up simply parroting what our competition is doing: advancing our position negligibly. By being exactly like all the other competitors, we naively participate in the parade of venders who are like the lemmings, blindly and without question, marching to the sea to their inevitable demise.

Like professional boxers, you cannot just be equal to the incumbent to be a challenger; you must be demonstrably better. Too often, salespeople are forcing their will and agenda on prospects before they have firmly established if their prospect has a compelling and driving reason to change. You cannot sell value until your prospect has voiced what value looks like to them.

Prospects do not buy in a vacuum where there are no other variables or priorities to consider, yet salespeople conduct themselves as if they did. Roughly 60% of all sales are lost to a "no buy" or "no change". Selling your value proposition does not account for the prospects who do not buy from anyone. Salespeople waste untold amounts of time and credibility establishing product superiority with a prospect who has not firmly decided they are truly committed to changing. They are trying to close someone Moses or the Prophet Mohammed could not close.

Like attracts like. Since we do not judiciously protect our information, prospects like-mindedly do not respect and treat our information as valuable. Loose lips not only sink ships, but they sink sales orders. We sell our products vigorously and then we buy them back. It is not unlike quicksand. The more we struggle and work to sell our products, the more we sink deeper into a giant black hole. How can we expect prospects to have an open mind when we feed them all our dogma? Without demonstrating and initiating a balanced approach, prospects will not feel obligated to treat us as equals.

Not only have salespeople commoditized their company's value proposition, they also have commoditized themselves. They look and sound like everyone else, yet wonder why it is so difficult for them to get new accounts, to get high-level meetings, and to have customers respect their time.

So long as we rely on our hollow dog-and-pony shows, we will be set up to be shot down like ducks in a row. As with certain diseases, the stronger the medicine we use to fight it, the more resistant the disease becomes. Feature and benefit selling by itself is the disease of which it is purported to be the cure. Prospects are resistant to your value pitch. The law of unintended consequences fits perfectly for feature and benefit selling. We are reduced to column fodder where prospects spreadsheet us and devalue our offering.

Feature and benefit selling is marginalized because we do not know what we are selling until we know what our prospects are buying, why they are buying, how they are buying, and when they are buying. Without these benchmarks being established, instead of getting active listening from our prospects, we get active annoyance. They are annoyed because being a product expert does not mean we are customer experts. When we recite volumes of technical information about our products, we are demonstrating we understand our own products, not our customer's business. We are essentially cutting off our nose to spite our face.

As you can pointedly see, all prospects are futures traders. They buy future expectations. No one buys the product for itself. We all buy it for what it can bring, but most salespeople are so in love with their offering, they are too busy to find out what the prospect is trying to accomplish and then help them navigate and define their options with a balanced assessment of the pros and cons.

The reason sales can appear to be so challenging and difficult is because we carry this heavy burden of proof around. The more we think we must sell our products' features and benefits, the less we will sell. It is a cruel joke of the universe. Ironically, the reason we do not change is because we would feel so guilty at how easy it is by not selling—it would grate against our Puritan work ethic. We would feel so cheated and shortchanged by patiently sitting back, listening, observing, questioning, and letting the prospect proactively do all the selling as to why or why not they would be open to changing. What would you do if you no longer had to be in charge? We take the path of most resistance because we feel in control, we hate to listen, we are self-absorbed, and we love to convince and persuade, even when it is not necessary.

As soon as salespeople conclude that they have nothing inherently special or unique to sell, that is when they will truly differentiate themselves from the competition and not have to rely on a flawed style of selling: features and benefits selling. We should no longer treat our product as if it were the means to an end. Our product and its attributes are simply a vehicle to help us build trust and respect by learning about our prospect's business. We should look at our products or services as an empty container. This container is inherently without value and it remains neutral until we start to fill it up with compelling and demonstrable proof and evidence as to why someone would want to change or buy. Today's salespeople can no longer be like Willie Loman in Arthur Miller's <u>*Death of a Salesman*</u>, who is out there gripping and grinning and telling and selling unsubstantiated and prejudiced features and benefits. Value based selling is fatally flawed because it fails to sufficiently address the two most important issues on any prospect's mind -- *"my personal agenda <u>and</u> my company's needs."*

9

Death of a Salesman

Traditional selling is built firmly on the foundation of confidence, boundless positive thinking, enthusiasm, unflagging persistence and always putting your best foot forward. This posture was effective in a bygone era where information was a powerful asset that salespeople brought to the table. In this marketplace, selling was predominantly a one-way street with information flowing from salesperson to prospect. Because information was relatively scarce and not always easily accessible, the salesperson's role revolved mostly around being a trumpet of product and service information. Their mandate was to get people to like them and then to persuade them of the superiority of their offering. This model became less relevant with the advent of the information age.

Now salespeople are faced with steep competition, rapid commoditization, less loyalty, customers who have global choices and who are more accountable to the bottom line, have less time for salespeople, and have quicker and greater access to information. Salespeople no longer have the luxury of establishing their worth by bringing valuable information to the marketplace.

Now their value is measured in their ability to bring creative problem-solving strategies to the table. Therefore, all the aforementioned traditional sales characteristics of enthusiasm, influence, persistence and boundless energy have been negated or neutralized.

In the information era, the selling skill sets and strategies that generate performance and create value are very different. Because of globalization and many other trends, the marketplace demands that salespeople be creative problem identifiers, business strategists and innovative problem-solvers. The sales skills necessary to execute this new strategy are: questioning and listening, patience, the power of suggestion, building strong business cases, being a change agent and advising and counseling as a business strategist. Diminished in value are product knowledge, proof of concept, educating customers and aggressive dogged determination in the face of insurmountable odds.

To facilitate this new selling strategy you need to take a non-selling posture. A non-selling posture projects a neutral objective position that allows your prospect to have the freedom to self-discover their own problems independent of your own agenda. The days of hard-charging salespeople with guns blazing, cajoling and persuading their customers to jump ship are obsolete and archaic.

Because your job is to educate your prospects on their problems and help them define their own options and solutions, you'll now have to rely heavily on questioning and listening skill sets to make you more productive and valuable.

To achieve understanding of your prospects' problems you'll also have to be very sensitive in providing a non-threatening environment where they feel they can share emotionally charged issues that are possibly latent and sensitive in nature. This is how you build strong business relationships that are created by care and understanding.

We have learned from NLP (Neurolinguistic Programming) that matching your prospect's posture is critical in trying to create an environment that is favorable to change. According to the latest research in NLP, if your prospect is negative, you must also be a bit negative. If they are angry about a service issue, you must certainly not initially appear rosy and optimistic even if you can resolve their complaint easily. This definitely goes back to my original premise that so often what prospects really want is to be heard, understood and listened to. The best resolution of a complaint or the best solution, if delivered too quickly without the prospect having the chance to vent or be heard, will consistently prove to be nonproductive and ineffective.

We all see this in our personal relationships every day. In relation to personal communication, what is the #1 complaint women have with men? You got it… *they don't listen.* But being an average guy I believe we do listen, we just don't give the impression that we took the time to really listen to what was said before we tried to give a quick suggestion or a fix. Women, like prospects, aren't looking for an answer as much as they are looking for someone who honors them by patiently listening and cares enough to allow them to get whatever they need off their chest. The "fixer" mentality doesn't work in personal relationships and its lack of success is even more amplified in sales.

Too often prospects would rather forfeit the assistance they need from salespeople than to do it on our terms. A good strategy to combat this hurdle is to extend a gesture of good faith by being the first to cede control. In doing so, one hopes to empower the prospect to follow suit.

The non-selling posture is the art of not knowing what anything means. This non-intuitive strategy is very disarming, impartial and lets the prospect always save face and maintain their dignity. It helps you to minimize the fear of the unknown for your prospect and gives them the permission and the space to say "no" and to hear and follow their own guidance.

You need to demonstrate faith and confidence in your prospect's ability to make decisions independent of your own agenda. The way you'll do this is by being detached from a positive outcome. The more needy and attached we are to a sale, the more blinded we are to the reality of our prospect's unique situation and needs. Prospects can sense this and this is why they can be very guarded with salespeople. So don't trespass upon the prospect's boundaries. Respect their boundaries and if they feel comfortable they may feel inclined to open up to you about their most pressing issues.

The non-selling posture will ultimately backfire and cause more harm than good if you use it as a slick selling technique without the authentic belief that you aren't here to sell and you are here to learn and understand. You ultimately will be perceived as manipulative and self-centered. If you adopt a non-selling posture and you truly believe in your heart that you aren't right for everyone, your price isn't worth it for everyone and your quality product is suitable only in certain circumstances, then you'll be perceived and trusted as an objective advisor and a nonbiased counselor working on behalf of your prospect's needs and not your own best interests.

10

The Giving of Good Listening Will Trump the Giving of Good Advice

The information economy has changed the profession of sales forever. In bygone years a salesperson could define their value through the unique quality and differentiation of their products and services. Today, with the abundance, ease and access to information, salespeople can no longer rely on their information to carry the day for them.

This seismic shift is forcing sales organizations to look at how they go to market and it is redefining their value proposition. Incidentally, most companies have made, at best, cosmetic changes and those who have are finding that their sales force is struggling with the implementation.

The only true differentiator that is sustainable for companies in defining their value is through their quality of engagement. Their value is now defined by getting information, instead of giving information. This puts all the focus on the prospect and totally deemphasizes the salesperson and their offering. And the tactic to implement the re-channeling of information is through the art of listening and asking thought-provoking questions.

Listening and questioning go hand-in-hand. In sales you can't do one without the other. I believe salespeople aren't necessarily bad listeners, but rather they are ineffective at asking questions that elicit important information that is worth listening to. So bad questioning is the real culprit in bad listening. If salespeople ask meaningful questions that elicit meaningful information they'd end up being great listeners overnight by default.

Salespeople too often are willing to only listen to themselves talk. Their intent isn't to learn and understand, rather to quickly get to the point where they can make their salient sales points. The best way to persuade is through listening and not through selling. This flies in the face of the way most salespeople sell. When was the last time you heard someone complimenting a potential salesperson by saying, *"You are a very good listener, you'd be great as a salesperson!"*?

To promote good listening, it is very important to take on a non-selling posture. A non-selling posture is all about putting all the focus on the prospect and having your product and solution taking a backseat.

The following are basic principles that make up the non-selling posture that promote and enhance active listening. Improve your questioning skills and your listening skills will improve exponentially.

- Your need to have people like you, and your need for approval will impede your confidence to ask thought-provoking questions.
- The most underrated and underutilized selling skill is the ability to find the truth. Finding the truth is a far more valuable skill set than selling and persuading.
- Salespeople who believe that their product information and solution are the least important part of the sales equation position themselves well as very caring listeners.
- Once you get good, you ask questions and listen intently more for the benefit of the prospect than for yourself.
- The best salesperson at the selling event is always the prospect. Let them internally sell themselves and then listen intently to how effective they are in selling you on changing.
- Need based selling is counterproductive. Prospects put more weight and value on what they want rather than on what they need. Listen intently more for wants than needs.
- Behavioral research states that 93% of communication is nonverbal. So all the talking you're doing instead of listening is having very little influence.

- Listen for personal and individual buying cues more so than corporate buying cues. Prospects buy individually and justify their buying decisions to salespeople corporately.
- Listen more for buying cues driven by problems, fear, dissatisfaction, loss and insecurity than for superficial reasons of gain, benefit, advantage, growth and opportunity.
- You are paid for your questions, not your answers.
- Listening is rewarded when you seek to understand before being understood, when you understand that it is more important to be interested than it is to be interesting, and when you realize that prospects don't care how much you know until you demonstrate first how much you care.
- Ironically, the more you tell the less you sell and the more you set yourself up for unfair comparison and objections. The less you tell the more you are forced to listen. Unlike selling, listening more effectively promotes trust.
- 5% of success in sales is based on closing. 95% of success is based on opening. Closing is a non-event. Opening is all about listening and questioning.

You're not in the business you think you are. Once you realize that, selling becomes much more strategic. For example; a software salesperson believes they are in the technology business and they position their product accordingly. They sell all the bells and whistles. However, their product should be positioned solely as a business solution. Their focus should be on operations, efficiency, profit, cost reduction and an overall business solution. Technology and software should be the furthest thing from their dialogue with their prospect.

So without anything to push, tout and drum, they're left with intense listening about the ins and outs of their prospect's business.

The combination of active listening and thoughtful probing negates the traditional reliance salespeople have on enthusiastic, eager, upbeat and can-do selling. How is it possible to probe deeply and listen intently in a diagnostic way for problems and pains without taking a sensitive, caring, introspective and pensive posture? Enthusiastic selling is the antithesis of selling by listening.

If prospects were really proficient in thoroughly understanding what their problems were, then listening wouldn't be as critical a skill set in selling. But in today's hyper changing, fast-paced and time-constraint driven environment, prospects are juggling so many balls at once, they don't have the luxury of focus that they did in the past. Hence, they rely on and value more than ever salespeople who can bring fresh insight and perspective to their business and their problems. Nothing accomplishes this strategy more effectively than a strategic thinker and listener.

11

No Problem is a Big Problem

Understanding what motivates prospects to change is the most important step in the sales process. Prospects always change for one of two reasons. The first reason is the justification for benefit, advantage and opportunity. The second reason is to avoid problems, fears, doubts, insecurities and dissatisfactions. The latter is what drives change. Psychological studies back this tenet up. It is basic human nature, whether making a personal commitment or a professional commitment to change, that we are more concerned and driven to first deal with loss versus opportunity. Only true visionaries and progressive entrepreneurs are driven by opportunity. However, behind all goals of opportunity rests the potential problem of not getting there. The pursuit of opportunity is an attempt to escape one's problems.

Behavioral scientist Abraham Maslow's research proved that people move faster away from problems, fear, insecurity than they will toward growth, opportunity and possibility. Prospects obviously are no different. They are far more likely to be emotionally attached to fear than opportunity. One sees this every day in the stock market. Investors are more emotionally involved in losing $10,000 than they are being overjoyed in gaining $10,000.

Let's pretend that I am a heroin user. It is wreaking havoc on my health, career, marriage and family life. My family intervenes and agrees to pay for the finest care money can buy. Can you guess why I am not going to take them up on this once in a lifetime offer? Because the suffering of going to rehab represents a greater suffering than that of a deadly heroin addiction. There is always a payoff for not changing and staying with the status quo.

Generally speaking, if you are happy and content, you don't strive to be happier. If you are full from a sumptuous four-course French meal, you don't keep looking for food to eat and satisfy yourself. However, what you will find are prospects who strive to guard and protect their state of being content and satisfied. And that is just another form of their problems. So within reason, some form of underlying fear, and discontent drives all action. Find it, uncover it, explore it, examine it and understand the level of intolerance and you are on the way to an easier life in sales. Keep in mind for most prospects, the truth and their reality are found in the heartfelt, the emotional, not in cold facts, figures, logic, rational and intellectual reasoning.

The challenge for most salespeople in making the transition from a product pusher to a change agent (strategic seller) is that it will require them to rely less on their personality and charm and more on their ability to ask thought-provoking questions and be patient listeners. For many salespeople this is a challenge because they love to talk and they tend to be very egocentric. The irony is, feature and benefit selling provides the exact opposite effect than is intended. Therefore salespeople must resist the temptation to sell at all costs.

Salespeople are not accustomed to giving up so much control and predictability in the sales cycle. Since the process relies so heavily on questions they feel uncomfortable with the fact that they can't control the answers and the different directions it may take them.

Be aware that the more problems they have, frequently the stronger the denial. So don't be frustrated when you run into denial. Many prospects would rather experience frustration and be in control and at least have it be predictable and manageable than change and feel out of control. There is always a payoff when in denial. By being attentive and inquisitive you give your prospect the greatest gift or compliment of being heard without you trying to fix or change anything. You allow them the respect and freedom to find their truth whether they buy or not.

Prospects maintain a strong identity with their viewpoints and problems. They frequently have a vested interest in the status quo. Things from the outside represent a threat. As a matter of fact salespeople represent problems in the eyes of prospects because no one savors change. Salespeople must find a way to include and acknowledge all the prospect's views and opinions. To accept their ideas is to show respect and trust. By taking this position you have nothing to prove and you build ultimate confidence with your prospects. That way, when you experience your ideas it will be easier for others to acknowledge, respect and act upon them. Prospects more often than not don't want to change because it is a known quantity. The devil you know is always better than the devil you don't know. Given the choice, most prospects are committed to the status quo because it is predictable and manageable. If they are not willing to admit to a problem or don't have one, then you have to make an important business decision as to what, if any, is your exit plan. You may decide to exit and reprioritize your prospect from an (A) to a (B) account. Or you may hang in there, knowing your chances are slim to nothing.

The process of helping your prospect find their problem is a self-initiation process for them. We create a safe space for them to make independent decisions as to whether change or not. That is why selling is a mutual examination of someone's ability to buy, change and act, rather than a process of persuasion. The salesperson becomes a conduit for the prospect to use for self-discovery. Helping the prospect understand the causes of their challenges takes incredible trust, rapport and relationship building skills. By being an instrument of change, salespeople provide a sympathetic ear, emotional support, an understanding of frustrations, and represent an opportunity for the prospects to collect their thoughts by talking the prospects through their issues. Prospects must have their problems thoroughly heard and understood in all its emotional and political complexities and as a precondition to have their problems solved before they will listen to the salesperson's advice. Jumping the gun and quickly going to a solution before the prospect has voiced all their issues is professional suicide for salespeople.

A lot of trust is also required for salespeople because they take on a non-selling posture of not having immediate answers for their prospects. This change agent mentality honors the prospect's independence to come to their own conclusions. When discussing problems the salesperson and the prospect ideally are equals. The salesperson helps the prospect stay focused and facilitates the prospect with the possible resistance or the coming to terms of the forthcoming change. This process requires a commitment to the truth and to being fully present. So salespeople have to put their own agenda to the side. The salesperson understands that both parties can decide not to participate if it is no longer useful or beneficial to either one of them. The prospect must be willing to take responsibility for the problem, and if there is too much resistance and push back, the salesperson can decide to opt out.

Most sellers fancy themselves as serving prospect's needs and objectives. But there is a huge incongruence between the belief, the skills, the strategies and the execution. Salespeople often are trying to solve problems that are not the real problems. One of the biggest frustrations in talking to customers about their problems is when you finally find a prospect who has legitimate actionable problems, only to learn after the fact that the deal fell through because of pre-existing political circumstances that the salesperson breezed over. As a change agent, your primary mandate is to determine if the conditions are ripe, favorable and conducive for your prospect to effectively and efficiently execute change.

If you adopted this non-selling posture you would never take your prospect's optimism and enthusiasm at face value. Instead you would recognize that the thinking that led them to be where they are needs to change before they would be ready to adopt anything different. To be an effective catalyst of change, it is important to understand all the variables around the environment that you will be selling into: Are they considering any other initiatives that will pre-empt your initiative? Or, maybe they are doing a manufacturing initiative and it is preoccupying all their time and focus. As you ask questions about the consequences of their problems and how it stacks up against other problems they are facing, you and your prospect can get your hands around the overall buying environment, the political nuances and the present conditions that may affect the implementation of your proposal. There is always a cost benefit analysis in relationship to change. Your job as a neutral change agent is to allow your prospects, in a safe environment, to self-discover, independent of your selling agenda, the cost of change and the cost of the status quo.

12

Persistence... The Final Myth: Just Say No

Salespeople are often faced with unresolved deals in their pipeline that they normally give up on or persist beyond any reasonable hope. There is a middle ground that is appropriate when you have reached the point of no return, your prospect is stringing you along in that they are taking you down the primrose path, and is not returning your repeated phone calls or emails.

You have to learn to let go and get closure on potentially bad deals that have gone way beyond their natural expiration date. This is hard for salespeople. As long as you believe that a good salesperson never quits, you will continue to have full pipelines of prospects who have a genuine, sincere interest in your product, but a passive and casual interest to act upon it. Good salespeople know where they can sell and when to quit. There are always two winners in a sales transaction. The first is the one who was awarded the contract. The second is the one who lost early, easily and effortlessly.

Closing the file allows you to preserve your self-dignity by receiving closure and gaining respect from prospects because you are willing to walk away.

Here are the key points and principles to be aware of and utilize when formulating your emails and voice mails when getting final closure:

- Tonality should be neutral, non-enthusiastic, warm and considerate
- If they are really interested they will not let you leave

- The more you make "no" available to your prospects, the easier it is for them not to have to use it: You essentially take the pressure off them
- By honoring their position and allowing them to come to their own conclusions, independent of your own agenda and influence, you build a future platform of trust and respect
- Take 100% responsibility for the lack of responsiveness of your prospects. Either you railroaded them into agreeing to be interested when they weren't or you were never on the right track to be privy to their priorities and their corresponding competing initiatives

A word of caution: don't have unrealistic expectations of prospects flocking to their computers or phones to return your call or email. Typically by the time you give the final closure message, your chances of revival have typically diminished tremendously. A return message of 10%-20% is average and can be expected in most industries.

The following are examples that you can snail mail, email, fax or leave as a voice mail:

- *"I've exhausted my repertoire of follow-up options. I sense that any more contact attempts on my part will be a nuisance to you, if it hasn't already. So, I don't want to waste any more of your time and patience. Could you give me the courtesy of leaving a message on my voice mail or email me as to what the status is? Thank you for your attention and consideration.*
- *"I've been trying to reach you for the past couple of weeks to no avail. I can safely assume you are busy and juggling many priorities. I know you are under no obligation to get back to me, but if you could send me an email as to where you stand on our proposal, I'd very much appreciate it. If I don't hear back from you I'll assume it is a dead issue and I'll take you off my active call list. Thank you for the courtesy."*
- *"You have asked me to do some work on your behalf and I have followed through on that request. I have left you numerous*

messages to provide you with that information and I would be greatly indebted to you for the courtesy of a return call. If I don't hear back, I will assume it is a dead issue and I will graciously take you off my active call list. Thanks."

- *"I want to hold up my end of the bargain by following up with you in good faith one last time. When we last met I believe I may have cornered you into agreeing to move forward, without giving you the option to do otherwise. I have been in the business long enough to know that when someone hasn't returned phone calls it is for a good reason. Could you extend me the professional courtesy as to where you stand? That way I can respect your time. If you are no longer interested, please give me a call to that effect. If I don't hear back from you by next week I'll graciously take you off my active call list."*

The following is additional verbiage you can use to add or replace from the proceeding examples. Guilt and shame are a subtle pretext that is imbedded in these examples. However, don't lay it on too thick or it will backfire:

- *"I wanted to hold up my end of the bargain by contacting you one last time."*
- *"I wanted to try to appeal to your sense of fair play and ask if you could give me closure, so that I don't overextend my welcome here."*
- *"In the spirit of fair play I wanted to give you the benefit of the doubt and call you one last time."*
- *"While it would be nice to do business with you, I'll respect your decision either way."*
- *"Any further calling on my part risks being a breach of professional conduct. If I don't hear back from you this week, I'll assume this is a dead deal and I'll cease any further efforts to contact you. If by chance you are still interested, don't hesitate to call me or email me."*

In sales it is crucial to realize that your job has more to do with getting people to make decisions and receiving resolution than it does in convincing and persuading. Therefore, you shouldn't feel apprehensive in getting prospects to give you a negative response. Getting closure allows you to emotionally move on and not be tied down with a pipeline of deals that are united by false hope.

Getting closure is a great strategy to keep your head in the game. By forcing the issue to get decisions or to make decisions for your prospects, you'll save yourself a lot of time and potential hassles. In sales there are always two winners; the one who was awarded the deal and the one who lost quickly, easily and with minimal expenditure of time, effort and resources.

13

Objection Prevention Trumps Objection Handling in Securing Appointments

I have more clients tell me if they could only get their salespeople to secure more appointments, it would greatly increase their company's performance. Usually it isn't for any lack of effort, or if it is, it is because their hit rate is so abysmal; they just gave up on trying. The problem is most salespeople aren't properly prepared and trained on how to handle common objections and stalls like *"send me some information"*; *"I'm too busy to meet"*; or *"call me back in 1 month to set up a meeting"*. Too often they try to sell the benefits of their product or service hoping to entice prospects to change their mind. Unfortunately, that usually isn't the real issue. The real issue is they want them to send information because they aren't interested at all or it is such a low priority for them it is only worth the impersonal and less time-consuming contact of email or snail mail. Most salespeople end up addressing the symptoms of sending information but not the real issues revolving around it. That's why it's trying and discouraging to nail down appointments.

The following are examples of questions and statements that attempt to isolate the real issues. Even when the following examples fail you, and they most assuredly will, they allow you a much better snapshot of how open and reasonable your prospect is. Half the battle of securing appointments is separating those who are willing and open to having dialogue versus those who aren't willing to be engaged and can't reasonably be converted. Keep in mind 95% of requests for literature is a total waste of your time.

Send Information

- *"I'd be more than happy to send you some information but I'm sure you can appreciate and understand that we are in the business of trust and confidence and if we are going to have any meaningful conversation or exchange of ideas, then we are going to need to meet. Does that sound fair and reasonable? I'm not coming in with any expectation of you changing. But I do want to meet you, shake your hand and find out if we could even be of help in the future."*

- *"Let me be very upfront with you. We do a lot of business with a lot of companies. We are also in the fortunate position that 95% of our business is with existing customers and referrals. I may not be able to help you, but I have found over the years in our business that it is critical for me to work very hard upfront to determine those who I can help and those who I can't. Those who I can help usually become long-term customers instead of one time deals because I've spent the time to learn about their business and their needs and then tailor a solution to fit their situation instead of trying to persuade them that what I have is what they need. So before we do anything like send you generic information, I need to believe I can help you and, most importantly, if you even need my help. And the only meaningful way to accomplish that is meeting personally. How does that sit with you?"*

- *"It sounds like you are uncomfortable in meeting with me. I can certainly understand. Do you mind if I ask, do you have a standing policy of not meeting with salespeople until they've sent you literature or do you have a policy of not meeting with salespeople on matters that are a low priority and of very little importance to you based on other more pressing initiatives?"*

The following question is good to ask to confirm that even if you did send the information as requested, your prospect most likely has little interest in further dialogue:

- *"If you were me selling you, would you follow up diligently after you sent the information or is your interest just passive and casual?"*

I'm Too Busy

The prospect's next favorite objection is, *"I'm too busy to meet you"*. Keep in mind, time is never the real issue, the real issue is you are not worth the time and more often than not based on their priorities, it is a legitimate objection. Therefore, try to isolate the real issue. Also make "no" an accessible answer so that you can further pinpoint whether they are being genuine and sincere in their intentions.

- *"Like you, my time is also very valuable. As a matter of fact, it is my most important asset. Prospecting represents only 10% of my time, so when I do it I must be certain I spend my time judiciously with qualified prospects. Let me share with you what, in my world, a prospect looks like and if you don't fit that description, I will graciously get out of your way. They are open-minded to the idea that their people could improve their skills because it is important for their company to maintain a competitive edge to continue growing. And most importantly, because this is a priority they are willing to meet with someone like myself, with the understanding and expectation that it might not go any further than an introductory meeting."*
- *"I know you are busy and I appreciate that and I hear that a lot. If I thought you had the time to meet with me, I'd have a minor seizure. The irony of our business is if you had the time you probably wouldn't be a very good prospect. I work with a lot of successful people like yourself who are very busy and I work with their schedules to find some holes in it. What holes can we find in your schedule?"*
- *"I may be sticking my neck out here, it probably isn't that you don't have the time, the real concern and issue is that you*

> *probably aren't convinced that I am worth the time and I may not be."*

- *"Are you busy very minute of the day, every week every month? Do you eat lunch? Take a coffee break? Can we meet before your day or after it?"*

Call me back in the Future

You'll also run into *"call me back in 1 month and I'll meet with you then"*, or some equivalent. A good strategy to employ here is bringing the future to the present. If they don't have a compelling reason to meet now, why will it change in one month?

- *"I'd be more than happy to call you back in 2 months. So that I respect your time, what will change in 2 months time where it will be worth your time to meet with me?"*
- *"I'd be happy to. Let me ask you a stupid question: when I call, will you take my call and if you are busy and not available, will you give me the courtesy of a return call? You are sure?"*
- *"Why don't you get out your calendar and let us set up something for that time. I sense if now isn't a good time then in 2 months it might also not be, due to your busy schedule. With all due respect, if you are unwilling to make this appointment, it might be because you've decided to get it over with now."*

Most objections are a symptom of another issue. Your goal is not necessarily to answer and address the objection, since you'll be answering, more than likely, a symptom. What you need to do is isolate and identify the real reason. Taking a relaxed and nonconfrontational posture is the most effective way in making your prospect feel non-threatened and respected. Your goal in dealing with objections is twofold: firstly, identify the authenticity of the objection; and secondly, determine the probability of overcoming it. By doing so, you increase the chances of your prospect answering and resolving their own issues and objections. Let them do some of the hard work.

14

Problem Killer Questions

The problem with presenting and selling solutions is that salespeople do it prematurely without firmly establishing whether a real problem exists enough to provide a prospect a compelling reason to change. The idea of selling problems instead of solutions also would be rendered unnecessary if prospects were always forthcoming, truthful, unguarded and not fearful of salespeople's hidden agendas.

The strategy of selling problems and their consequences is typically employed most effectively early on in the sales engagement. It works particularly well on the phone to try to secure appointments with hardened and skeptical prospects. It is also effective with initial face-to-face meetings where the prospect easily granted you an appointment without articulating any noted problems. We've all been faced with prospects who for no apparent reason take time out of their busy day, grant you an appointment and then they are silent and unwilling to have any kind of meaningful dialogue.

These scenarios are familiar and typically come to a standstill when prospects give salespeople flimsy, wishy-washy noncommittal responses that have no weight to them, such as: *"we are always open to new ideas, tell me what you have for me, what's new, we are very happy but we like to keep our options open, and, if we saw something really exciting we definitely wouldn't rule it out."* These prospects are the toughest to sell because they at face value have no compelling reason to change.

The strategic flaw most salespeople have at this stage is that instead of probing for potential gaps and problems, they believe they've been granted a temporary license to kill. They get out their feature and benefit machine gun, lock and load, and pray and spray, leaving carnage of worthless and wasted information. In other words, they prematurely sell their solution without having the faintest idea what problem they are trying to solve or fix.

Salespeople frequently sell like this because they are under the grand illusion and spell that their value propositions and their information will carry the day and ultimately result in a sale. They need to be aware that unless a prospect has a problem with meaningful consequences, the likelihood of change is slim to nothing. That is why your mandate is not to provide solutions but rather to isolate and identify problems.

The old adage, that you can lead a horse to water but you can't make it drink, is relevant to the strategy of using problem prompters. However, making prospects drink is not your priority. What you need to do is to make them thirsty, but at the same time create reasonable doubt, problems and insecurity. Turning a prospect's complacency into an actionable desire represents the true art of selling. Anything short of this, you are working too hard for your own good.

In order to get problems you must give problems. This means that if your goal is to get prospects to open up and share their problems or doubts, you are going to have to proactively initiate dialogue by posing questions that are designed to elicit emotional responses. The way you achieve this is to craft questions that zero in on not what you sell, but the problems you solve and the corresponding negative consequences they create. By framing questions in hypothetical language, using emotional metaphors, you are hoping to engage your prospect with questions that get to the core of why people change, which is always emotionally and intuitively, instead of logically and intellectually.

The reason you use hypothetical language is because it is less threatening and less direct and the prospect usually feels less compelled to be defensive. Metaphors or phrases are effective to use because they tend to emotionally involve a prospect with language that is more charged with feelings than normal staid intellectual language. Example: *"Do you ever have prospects who string your salespeople along, create false hope and constantly lead your people down dead end detours that have them jumping through hoops and wasting their time?"* You can probably guess the aforementioned is more effective than saying, *"Do you experience prospects who don't make decisions promptly therefore lengthening your sales cycles?"* Careful selection of the right words and proper phrases can be worth a 1,000 pictures.

I look at problem prompter questions as a litmus test. You create a menu or a problem chain of questions and statements that, through a process of elimination, leads your prospect through a series of worst case scenarios that they might be experiencing, have experienced or are worried about experiencing. If they are in denial or actually aren't having any problems what do we now know? They more than likely aren't a good prospect for the immediate present and you more than likely will need to de-prioritize them or re-categorize them.

In my training sessions, getting my customers to start formulating these questions can become very difficult, because when I ask them to list out in order all the biggest challenges, problems, irritants and insecurities that their prospects experience or have shared with them, I usually get a roomful of blank stares. Guess why? They are so product-centric that they aren't accustomed to looking at their prospects' business from their perspective. Salespeople need to now be category or industry experts on the prevailing problems and frustrations their prospects experience. You can also do this by job functions and title.

However, don't be naive in thinking that all your prospects are going to be enthusiastically engaged. Be as nurturing, neutral, doubting and disassociated as possible when you deliver these powerful questions. This strategy helps to neutralize resistance and soften the blow of your direct questions. Avoid at all costs coming off as an interrogator or a hard-nosed lawyer who is badgering the witness. Problem prompter questions empower your prospect by engaging them and focusing all our attention on them. If you find yourself in a bind, where you can't remember your problem prompter questions, just fall back or default to your old features and benefits by just changing one thing. After you have enumerated your features and benefits simply ask them if any of those issues are important to them. And, if they say yes, ask them why. Although not even remotely as effective, it still gives you a chance to get the ball rolling especially if you are new to this concept of selling.

The following are examples of questions and statements that locate and identify problems. They are divided into questions specifically to isolate prospects who may have problems with an existing supplier, prospects who aren't doing business with anyone yet (competition is the status quo), and questions to uncover problems with an existing supplier but formulated in the positive instead of the negative.

Problem Prompter Questions and Statements with Existing Supplier

The first examples are a series of questions which seek to uncover gaps and problems with an existing supplier. These questions are universal, generic and will fit just about any product or service, in just about any business relating to almost any general problem. Obviously these are concept questions and can be tailored to fit your unique situation.

- *"They are real efficient with conventional orders, but they lack the depth of offerings to be an efficient one-stop shop and therefore they are adding to your costs of acquisition."*
- *"They work real well with big customers but they don't give enough personal care to smaller accounts that are strategically less important to them. Hence, the smaller accounts get lost in the shuffle sometimes."*
- *"They over-manage the account, they are a pest and unprofessional and are always badgering their customers inappropriately to order more."*
- *"They are competitive on large orders but on smaller or unusual orders that are very expensive and cumbersome to deal with."*

- *"Their quality is generally good, but it hasn't evolved and kept up with the new cutting edge technology in the industry and therefore it is slower and more inefficient."*
- *"They are constantly going through changes of management, salespeople, ownership or technology platforms, making it very difficult to get things done through them efficiently and easily."*
- *"Do you ever have lingering questions in the back of your mind as to whether their high prices are justified?"*
- *"Do you ever find after a successful implementation of their solution, you are left with a bad taste in your mouth because there is sloppy and inconsistent billing that causes logjams and extra layers of bureaucracies?"*
- *"They do a real good job of fixing issues and problems and generally are very responsive. However, it is irritating because the problems continue to recycle and repeat themselves."*
- *"Do you run into the scenario where your vendor doesn't own up to the responsibility to have solid contingency plans in place so they can nip problems in the bud before they happen or get out of control?"*
- *"Do you have any concerns that without a strong backup supplier that you aren't always able to keep your existing supplier honest and keep them hustling for you?"*
- *"Sometimes I hear companies are very faithful and loyal to the years of good service that their vendor has provided, however, recent developments have them question their longer term viability and their ability to meet your own business requirements and needs. And you aren't sure you have the luxury to ride out the storm with them because you have too much at stake."*
- *"They don't take the time to really learn about your business and they aren't technically proficient and knowledgeable about your business and you end up using a lot of your valuable time and resources making up for this shortfall."*
- *"They are really good at fulfilling local orders but don't have the size, national reach and buying power to help you nationally and globally."*

- *"They are efficient with long lead times but when you need expedited orders right away, they drag their feet and are slow to get back to you with updates and they too often leave you in a lurch."*
- *"They have very attractive front end pricing, but the back end costs of late deliveries, shoddy service and inconsistent and unreliable quality really wipe out any cost savings."*
- *"They do a very good job consistently in the easy transactions. But anything that is not cookie cutter they over promise and under deliver."*
- *"Do you ever find that your salesperson is likeable and well intentioned but is just a glorified order taker who can't solve real problems or resolve customer service issues because they don't have any clout in their company to get things done?"*
- *"Do you experience frustration with your salesperson who is Johnny on the Spot when taking orders from you but when you need them to get you quick answers they are too busy, they can't be bothered or they are always making excuses?"*
- *"They aren't bringing you innovative ideas and programs to make you more competitive. They push the same old time-honored, tried and true ideas and they don't think outside the box."*

Problem Prompter Questions and Statements with a Positive Spin with Existing Supplier

The next series of questions and statements are a mirror image of the first series but with a positive spin on the problem. You will sometimes find that prospects won't admit to problems, but are open to admitting to imperfections. This is a more advanced way of questioning that requires a bit more sophistication and practice. The advantage with this line of questioning is you aren't probing for problems so much as you are making statements to confirm they don't have problems and their situation is satisfactory, ideal and representing the best case scenario. Because some of these scenarios aren't totally realistic, you will have to be very nonchalant, neutral and objective when you present them.

Prospects who tell you emphatically they are happy, things are great and they would not consider changing typify these examples. Because of the strong nature of prospects' convictions and beliefs, these questions and statements will often prove to be unsuccessful in forwarding your agenda and cause, but will be effective in saving you time and resources on not pursuing lost causes.

These positive problem questions or problem prompters hope to sanitize and whitewash their problems so thoroughly that no reasonable prospect can agree to this picture- perfect world you are describing.

The following are examples you can use that really put the rubber to the road and have you placing stark realities right in front of them to chew over and consider.

- *"Your rep is very proactive and anticipates problems before they get out of hand."*
- *"Your rep is very informed and knowledgeable with your business and can help you define your needs and provide viable solutions quickly and with great understanding."*
- *"They are flexible and willing to go beyond the call of duty when needed."*
- *"If they run into problems they take responsibility for their mistakes and quickly provide options."*
- *"They keep in touch with you regularly and in a professional manner without being a pest."*
- *"You are getting things on a timely basis without having to chase down and micromanage your orders."*
- *"Their quality is consistent and reliable."*
- *"Your rep has the clout to get things done and expedite when you find yourself in a time crunch or bind."*
- *"They have technical expertise and knowledge to understand your problems so you are confident they'll get it right the first time without you having to reeducate and re-explain everything to them."*

- *"They are easy to do business with because they have multiple offices nationally and global capabilities."*
- *"They can handle local small orders as well as complex global orders."*

Problem Prompter Statements for Prospects who are Non-users and not actively in the Marketplace

The final series of problem prompters are for situations where your prospect is not a current user of what you sell and therefore obviously they are not using any supplier. You can't ask the aforementioned problem prompters because they are 100% geared towards up-seating an existing supplier. Hence, the scenario of problem prompters with non-users requires more creativity and conceptual selling because you have a prospect who is more than likely not in the market, isn't actively looking for solutions in this area, may not be aware that any problems exist and may not be aware that there is even existing technology out there to help them. However, the beauty of new application opportunities is when approached properly, there is no competition, little comparison and accessibility to price checks is limited. The highest margins are available in selling to prospects who aren't actively in the market. The bad news is, these prospects take more time to locate and must be sold at a higher level.

The following are questions to uncover problems with the status quo. Keep in mind, like the two earlier examples: there is never any mention of what you can do for your prospect, why you may have a superior offering or what they have to gain by considering changing. The focus now is all on your prospect and their potential problems. What you can do for them at this stage is irrelevant and unimportant. The only thing that is consequential at this stage is having your prospect admitting to a problem and deciding if it is worth addressing. This is where salespeople have to transition from product and solution providers to business strategists and change agents. Once again your mandate is to isolate and define problems, not solve them. Once you've done a thorough job of defining the problem, the solution becomes a nonevent.

- *"They are running into time constraints and time is being swallowed up because they are being pulled in so many directions with fewer resources and manpower to draw upon."*
- *"They find they have plenty of time and expertise to do it internally but at the cost of misallocating valuable and expensive personnel who could be doing other projects with a greater return on investment."*
- *"Their people are so busy doing other important and pressing things that they don't have the time, interest or inclination to stay current with all the changes happening in their industry. Consequently they aren't learning and staying current with the new technology to efficiently perform in the area."*
- *"They are finding that the upfront costs appear to be inexpensive to do it internally but when you add up all the incidental costs on the back end, they are being penny wise and pound foolish."*
- *"They've hit a wall or a point of diminishing returns with their own resources. They keep doing the same thing or worse yet trying new things and getting the same results and they can't grow or move on to the next level."*

Probing questions and statements that prompt problems or admission of non-ideal circumstances are a far superior method of selling than the traditional feature and benefit style of selling. What makes it so difficult for salespeople to make this transition is that the sale is no longer about them, their company, and their superior offering. Because most salespeople are egocentric, self-consumed and product-focused, they have a hard time relinquishing this self-centered strategy of providing information and solutions. Once they take a non-selling posture that is objective and non-biased, they will find that they can more quickly identify if prospects have a compelling reason to change.

15

Problem Locator Questions

Since for all intents and purposes prospects could care less about you and your company, the problem locator questions are a great way to put all the emphasis and focus on prospects. These questions are an excellent tool to use to build rapport; create a long-term relationship built on trust and confidence; build a business case instead of just a product justification; and save time, energy and resources by quickly identifying your prospect's problems, consequences, commitments, priorities and motivations to change.

The depth of these questions underscores the tenet that there are many ways to skin a cat. I have listed, obviously more than necessary, the questions you may use to gain insight and understanding of your prospects' problems. Generally 5-10 questions will suffice. When I have my clients in my training sessions list out all their own diagnostic questions, they can usually go no deeper than 2 questions, if that! The process of asking these in-depth questions is essentially alien to them. The beauty of these questions is that it forces you to do all the things that make a great salesperson: empathize, listen, demonstrate care and expertise, and most importantly, exude trust.

These questions are to follow when a prospect states a problem or a concern in their business. Your job as a salesperson is to understand the full extent of your prospect's problems and help them understand if the timing is right for them to act on it.

To make it a little easier to understand the flow and strategy of these questions, I've loosely categorize them into three areas:

1. Big picture and defining the problem.
2. Consequences and implications.
3. Next step, commitment and options.

1. Big Picture and Defining the Problem

- *"What is your stake or vested interest in fixing the problem?"*
- *"In relation to this problem or situation, how are you evaluated?"*
- *"When you went to your existing suppliers and shared your frustrations about this problem, what reassurances did they give you that it wouldn't be repeated?"*
- *"What are some of the original causes of the problem?"*
- *"When you are saying it is a problem, what standard are you using to measure it against?"*
- *"Why do you think the problem has been going on for so long?"*
- *"When do you need the problem fixed by?"*
- *"Is the timing right for you to stick your neck out and champion this cause?"*
- *"What could you have done to avoid this problem?"*
- *"What kind of return or payoff will you be looking for if you get a successful resolution of the problem?"*
- *"How is your job performance measured in relation to this issue?"*
- *"What evidence do you have that this is a problem? Is it quantifiable or soft evidence?"*
- *"What do you have riding on this if it is successful or unsuccessful?"*
- *"Is it important to get quantifiable evidence to justify a change?"*
- *"How often do you think the problem has come up where you weren't even aware of it?"*
- *"Who is ultimately responsible for this?"*
- *"How acceptable or unacceptable is this problem?"*

- *"Beyond job satisfactions and pride in doing a job well, what, if anything, do you have riding on this problem? Is that enough to carry the day?"*
- *"Why have you been dealing with this for so long?"*
- *"Why do you think it is happening? Who is responsible?"*
- *"What's your role in this problem?"*
- *"When you told your people in your department that this is unacceptable, what did they say?"*
- *"What bothers you the most about this problem?"*
- *"How can you cost-justify fixing this?"*
- *"In the meantime, what are you doing to compensate for this problem?"*
- *"Prior to our meeting, this was a latent back burner issue. Now we're looking at it to determine if it will be a front burner issue. How are you going to rectify this?"*
- *"How are your going to break the news to your department that this is no longer acceptable?"*
- *"What has prevented you from fixing this in the past?"*
- *"What kind of timeframe are you working in to fix this?"*
- *"I'm hearing it is a company problem or industry problem, but I'm not hearing it as your problem."*
- *"What is management's contribution to this problem?"*
- *"Who else is aware of it?"*
- *"What is your strategy to fix this problem?"*
- *"Who supports this action?"*
- *"Specifically, what success criteria will you be looking for beyond an increase in revenue? How big of a measurable change will you be looking for in your business? Will you have the time to drive this and monitor it?"*
- *"Is this problem causing other problems?"*
- *"What practical options do you have to address this?"*
- *"What are the key performance indicators for your business to run profitably, and how is this impacted by the problem?"*
- *"What kind of pressure is this causing you and the business?"*
- *"Does your competition have these problems?"*

- *"When you compete, how do these problems manifest themselves?"*
- *"Have you told your customer the problem will be fixed? Have you told your General Manager that the problem won't continue?"*
- *"Who will ultimately have responsibility for the successful resolution of this problem?"*

2. <u>Consequences and Implications</u>

- *"You are a successful company. How did you get yourself in this mess?"* (a personal favorite of mine)
- *"What issues must be addressed first in order to seriously consider changing or fixing this problem?"*
- *"What political issues must be addressed before you decide to change?"*
- *"What is it about your company's culture that allows this problem to persist unimpeded?"*
- *"What is your greatest fear about addressing this problem?"* (Get the worst-case scenario and/or the best-case scenario.)
- *"If this problem is solved, does it free up your time to pursue other priorities or initiatives?"*
- *"Are there any competing initiatives or projects that could take precedence over this?"*
- *"Have you exhausted all options in trying to fix this yourself?"*
- *"You succeeded in the past without this, what makes you believe you need it now?"*
- *"What could you have done to avoid this?"*
- *"If they haven't been able to fix your problem, what makes you believe someone else can have better luck?"*
- *"Have you made the decision that you have to do something with somebody to address this issue?"*
- *"Realistically, when is the most practical time to deal with this?"*
- *"Is this the right time to stick your neck out and do something different?"*

- *"Compounded by the number of incidents where the problem resurfaces, multiplied by the number of salespeople you have, adding the cumulative effect of time span of the problem, what are the costs?"*
- *"What else is going on with your company that could possibly take precedence over this?"*
- *"Is there a sense of urgency to fix it or do you have plenty of breathing room?"*
- *"If it continues at this rate or pace and goes unchecked, at what point do you decide it has to change?"*
- "If we hadn't had the opportunity to meet, what would you have done to address this problem?"

3. Next step, commitment and options

- *"What hurdles or risks do you see in moving forward to fix this problem?"*
- *"From your perspective, what is the next step for you?"*
- *"With or without us, have you made a final decision that you must fix the problem?"*
- *"I'm wondering if you get some measure of security by letting this problem go unchecked?"*
- *"How will you know who has the best solution for you?"*
- *"It seems like you are invested in keeping things the way they are?"*
- *"How would you know that a solution was successful? Where would it show up?"*
- *"What performance indicators will increase or decrease if we are successful?"*
- *"How will you measure success?"*
- *"What kind of payoff will you be looking for?"*
- *"What's the value of this problem over time?"*
- *"So far, what conclusions have you reached about fixing this problem?"*
- *"How do you see us helping you, and why us as opposed to someone else?"*

- *"Let's imagine the problem is fixed. What would it look like and how would you know?"*
- *"How confident are you that this will work?"*
- *"From a timing perspective, what makes this a particularly attractive or unattractive time to address this?"*
- *"What is the date by which you hope to get the results in place?"*
- *"What has to be in place for this deal to go down smoothly?"*
- *"Assuming you make a change, what concerns would you have about the implementation step?"*
- *"If you could design the perfect solution, what would it look like, how much would you spend and how long would it go for?"*
- *"For all the good you are trying to achieve, do you see any unavoidable negative consequences?"*
- *"What sense of urgency do you have here?"*
- *"Have you decided yet that this is the best approach to address this issue?"*

The key with these problem locator questions is to take a non-selling posture and allow the prospect to self-discover their own issues and problems and grant them the freedom to come to their own conclusions regardless of your selling agenda. These questions are effective because they demonstrate very little self-interest and put all the focus and attention on the prospect and the truth.

16

Sell Like a Business Owner

Successful and productive salespeople sell as if they were a business owner or CEO. They apply a strict return on investment mentality on all of their activity. They also manage their company's assets as if they were their own. Salespeople who take on a business owner mentality view their territory or account base as their own company where they have total fiscal responsibility. Even though they may be salaried employees, they act as if they were an enterprising entrepreneur or someone who is on straight commission. The litmus test or desirability metrics they use to assess their activities is: If I had to put my own skin in the game, if I had to cover my own salary, benefits and expenses, would I feel comfortable investing it all in this deal? Asset management is just good governance.

John Hirth of Selling Dynamics, a former colleague and mentor, originally created this concept of CEO mentality. He recognized the importance of salespeople having full fiscal responsibility for their day-to-day activities.

When we created our sales methodology we decided to model the best practices of business owners and apply them to sales. In our research, we found that business owners were very effective in managing and controlling the key assets in their own business. They not only applied these assets to the operating side of their business, but also to the sales side.

In our findings, we discovered that business owners, when put into a sales role, were effective while selling, not because they were necessarily good salespeople, had good sales strategies, or were great at building rapport, but rather because they were masters of managing their assets. They knew when and under what circumstances to allocate their valuable assets to get an optimal return on their investment.

They knew that their assets of intellectual capital, time, trust, company resources, and self-concept/confidence were their leverage and control points in a sale.

Salespeople who adopt a business owner mentality judiciously guard and protect these assets and allocate them in a very selective manner. Their assets are their currency and capital. Through a balance/gain equation, they evaluate every opportunity for risk and reward. They are not only good asset managers, but they are also good risk managers. They apply sound oversight principles to all of their investment strategies.

The following is a description of each of the five assets:

Time is money. Time is a depreciating asset. Once you lose it you can never get it back. Too many salespeople make the fatal error of confusing managing their calendar and planning their week with time prioritization. After carefully examining their calendar, it wouldn't be unusual to find that they logistically organized their week very diligently with activity that was low yielding and with prospects who were low probabilities.

Somebody once told me that time kills all deals. This was a very valuable lesson for me because I operated under the exact opposite assumption. My deluded belief was the longer they sat out there, the greater the chance I had to patiently hang in there, out-distance the competition, make a lasting impression with my prospect about my commitment and get them to feel a strong connection to me. I believe most salespeople feel compelled to be persistent, even at the cost of wasting their time, because it is the only option they have because they have poor selling skills. Poor use of time is definitely a symptom of lack of an effective sales process. The following reinforce this concept:

- There are always two winners at the selling event. The first winner is the salesperson who was awarded the business. The second winner (silver medalist) is the salesperson who lost quickly, easily, and effortlessly with expending minimal energy and time.
- The most underrated and underutilized sales skill today is knowing when to walk away. Salespeople who practice a business owner mentality know that selling is a game of efficiency. Learning to cut your losses is a great way to utilize time. You protect your asset of time when you realize selling is not only who to sell, but who not to sell.
- A lot of time is wasted and poorly allocated because of avoidance activity. Because salespeople generally loathe prospecting, they will spend an incredible amount of time chasing, groveling, and inappropriately following up on the same group of prospects who give them glimmers of false hope or throw them occasional bones, because the alternative is even more painful… prospecting. Wasting one's time not only provides a false sense of security, it also provides a safe haven from prospecting.

One of the biggest complaints I hear from salespeople is the fact that prospects don't respect their time. The reason they don't respect their time is because salespeople demonstrate that they don't respect their own time. Until salespeople respect their own time, they can't reasonably expect that their prospects will respect their time.

In real estate, the mantra is location, location and location. In sales, the mantra is timing, timing and timing. Whether it is your information or your resources, proper timing and allocation will determine your yield or your percentages. Time your solutions when prospects are in a position to make decisions. Anytime before that, you put your time asset at risk.

The asset of time is also misappropriated when you over-rely on transactional selling. This style of selling is hugely time-consuming and costly. You incur the direct costs of selling over and over again each time prospects present you with an opportunity, as opposed to strategic selling, which is efficient and keeps down your costs of sales.

Intellectual Capital. Information is your intellectual capital. A salesperson with a business owner mentality plays their cards close to the chest and judiciously guards and protects their information and dispenses with it sparingly. You allocate your information when your prospect is in a position to make decisions. Your information represents your leverage and control points in the sales cycle. In the past, salespeople's value was firmly established by the information they brought to the table. The information economy has changed all that. Since information is accessible freely and widely, salespeople's value proposition has been neutralized and marginalized. Salespeople's mandate now should be to get information, not give it. This totally changes the dynamics of a typical sales call.

You are now paid and rewarded for your questions, not your answers. No longer can you afford to build a product case. You have to build a business case, which is heavily influenced by your ability to garner important, privileged and sensitive information from your prospect.

Selling is more about what you don't know versus what you do know. The prospect's information carries the most weight. Yet, salespeople act as if their information is king and they invariably overplay their hand, in turn diminishing the importance and dignity of their prospect.

Trust. People buy from people they like. This used to be the old relationship tenet. Today, it has shifted to people buy from people they like, but far more importantly, they buy from salespeople who have the expertise, the patience, and the understanding to learn about their business in a way that no other salesperson could match. In other words, people they trust. Hence, the salesperson with the best understanding of the customer's business will consistently outsell the salesperson with the best solution.

Many salespeople fancy themselves as consultive sellers who build strong relationships. However, the reality is that many salespeople are merely empty suits. They are often goodwill ambassadors and overpaid customer service reps who do not bring substance to the party beyond good service, attention to detail and good follow up with a friendly and sunny disposition.

Due to the universal parity in products and services, salespeople's ability to build trust and long-term relationships is their only remaining differentiator. Trust is the ability to build relationships and the skill to engage prospects at a deeper level. This happens to be the most sustainable competitive advantage companies have over one another in today's marketplace.

To build trust you must first extend it. Trust is created when the salesperson puts their self-interest aside and honors their prospect's freedom and independence to self-discover their own answers and conclusions, independent of the salesperson's personal agenda.

Resources. Your resources are anything that costs your company money that you allocate to customers. Most salespeople's behavior reflects the belief that their company has infinite resources. One resource that is constantly misallocated by salespeople is manpower. Ask yourself, how often do you do flimsy quotes and proposals that are prepared by estimating or by the technical department without any consideration to cost? If you were the owner of your own company and you had to pay all those direct costs out of your pocket, you would probably think long and hard about it.

Your resources are your leverage. Allocate them according to when you can optimize your position. Look at your resources as an investment. Would I invest in this account if I knew I was vulnerable to a low probability of return? One of my machine tool distributors built a $500,000 state of the art demo room. The first month, they were ecstatic with the activity it generated. Unfortunately, they soon realized that salespeople booked the room with tire kickers and their two top producing salespeople couldn't schedule their two best accounts in for that month. Granted, they sold them the next month, but it did increase their cost of sales because their salespeople were not utilizing their leverage.

Salespeople should guard their resources not because they are good corporate citizens concerned with costing the company money, rather they should guard their resources because it is their control and leverage point in the sale. Salespeople should adopt an owner mentality because if they allocate their resources wisely and accordingly, it will personally make them more productive and efficient. Ironically, what is good for the goose is good for the gander.

One should have a desirability matrix to use on all prospects who are tapping your company's resources: do they qualify for your resources and what is the likelihood of a positive return on that investment?

Self-Concept/Confidence. One's self-concept is one of the most important assets salespeople need to guard and protect. Without confidence and a healthy self-esteem, the other four assets predictably will be severely neutralized.

Salespeople will generate results at a level consistent to their own self-worth. In sales, your self-worth is controlled and defined in part by your own rejection/success ratio and the resulting thought process that follows it. One is easier to control and manage than the other.

The only way to manage rejection is to be more discerning and discriminating as to whom you make an offering. Rejection would play a lesser role in sales if salespeople were far savvier about pursuing high percentage business, in lieu of pie in the sky opportunities. Salespeople who adopt a business owner mentality always factor in their self-worth, passion and emotional expense when assessing the viability of deals.

The need for approval can be very devastating to one's self-esteem. Salespeople with a high need for approval set themselves up for high levels of rejection because they are unwilling to risk the approval of their prospects by asking tough questions. They tend to get used and reduced to free consultants. Be aware that no one can give you approval but yourself. Ironically, seeking approval from others prevents us from recognizing and experiencing it in ourselves.

17

"Show Me The Money!"

Most salespeople build their case around the idea that if the funds are there they can be allocated. In some cases, they've got the money; they just aren't going to spend it with you. I'm reminded of an early experience in my career when I was calling on Microsoft. When I asked them what their budget was for training, they responded rather smugly and said, *"Rick, don't worry, we are Microsoft, and there is plenty of money."* What I failed to ask in my naiveté was, *"Is there any for me?"* and unfortunately there wasn't. You'll find some prospects have deep pockets, but short fingers. They'll tell you not to worry, the money is there. But "there" is where it stays and you aren't getting any of it.

In order to be an effective agent of change, salespeople have to factor into their sales strategy the idea that prospect's decision to change (allocating money, time and resources) is a full integration of human capital, operational resources, fears, priorities and initiatives, timing and available bandwidth and share of mind all bundled up into a complex package. It is the job of the salesperson and the prospect to mutually self-diagnose the possibilities and hurdles. Unless they can comfortably come to terms and manage all these disparate variables, change will be stifled.

In our sales process, the investment step follows the initial step of finding pain and problems. Assuming they have pain, our goal now is to determine if they can spend the money to fix the problem and to make sure the timing and resources are properly aligned to facilitate change.

Questions to ask to initially determine their budget

- *"How were you planning to fund this investment?"*
- *"What are you authorized to spend?"*
- *"In your company, if you have a problem that is costing you two million dollars, what is considered an acceptable investment to address a number like this?"*
- *"Have you made any mental calculations as to how much this is going to run you? Can you share it?"*
- *"You aren't going to shock me and tell me you have an idea as to how much this is going to cost you?"*
- *"Have I earned the right yet to ask you what your budget is?"*
- *"Do we have enough trust here for me to ask you what your budget is?"*

Second round of questions to ask when you get push back

- *"How did you get your figure?"*
- *"So is there any wiggle room or flexibility on $350,000 since that is the low end of our offering?"*
- *"The good news is I can help you. The bad news is it is going to cost you more."*
- *"I'm guessing you have an unlimited budget and I'm free to use as much as humanly possible? So since you don't, could you share your range with me?"*
- *"Is it important enough for you to share with me what you were hoping to spend so I have some guidance in what to recommend to you?"*
- Write down on a piece of paper what you charge. Flip it downwards and ask the prospect to tell you what their budget is. This will only work if you do it with lightness and have established a very strong rapport with your prospect.

To effectively execute the investment step you need to ask how your solution will be integrated into the prospect's existing workflow or process. You need to go beyond just the functional criteria and address external criteria. What internal changes must be made, what accommodations need to happen to have a smooth transition? In real estate it is location, location and location. In sales, it is timing, timing and timing. You must put out on the table all potential conflicts of interests, unfinished business, cultural clashes, unresolved issues and possible competition or power struggles. For limited and scarce resources, salespeople are generally so one-dimensional and single-focused on their quest to close that they seek positive outcomes for themselves at the expense of their prospect. When you are selling your solution to a company you are competing with everything and everyone. You are fighting not only for their time and attention, but also against all their personal and professional distractions. Because there are so many variables in the investment step, it is rarely black and white and cut and dried. So often it isn't a question of whether it is a good investment or if the timing is right, it is a question of where they could potentially spend the time, money and resources elsewhere to get a better payoff.

Frequently your biggest competition is a huge and formidable competitor that you totally don't take into account. That company is SQI or Status Quo Inc. In many cases you have competition you are never aware of: new fleet of trucks, two weeks of vacation, new accounting system, coaching Little League baseball and a pending plant relocation. Make sure you really understand all the variables involved that could re-channel your prospect's attention. From the prospect's perspective, every change is viewed as an opportunity or a possible threat.

Effective change agents cover all their bases and are able to chart the flow of critical prospect business functions and their effects. They have a good handle on the big picture and the current initiatives and priorities. Once you uncover all the unidentified obstacles and have a handle on all the variables, find out what their timetable is for execution of change. Understanding how the change will be integrated into your prospect's business allows you to help your prospect come to terms with all the necessary contingencies and potential disruptions. There is always a transition cost associated with change so make sure you get your prospect to get all their ducks in a row to ensure the process goes smoothly.

18

The Way You Buy is a Leading Indicator for the Way You'll Sell

Price

Price is never the real issue for prospects. The reality is that many times your product and service isn't worth the price. Not because it doesn't justify itself, but because your prospect doesn't value it. So instead of constantly fighting price, focus your time positioning your product with prospects who are aligned with you price point or your value proposition.

Let's first take a look at the most important contribution as to why salespeople get caught up in the price game themselves. Salespeople are their own worst enemy. Without question, salespeople pin themselves into a corner with their hard-won attitudes, beliefs, and personal buying habits that don't support them selling value.

Personal Buying Habits

Birds of a feather flock together, like attracts like. The best way to change your own selling habits is by modifying your own buying habits. Performance value shoppers tend to attract higher-end buyers. By becoming a quality value shopper you will begin to naturally assume a different selling posture that will draw like-minded prospects.

Selling Habits and Buying Habits

The following are leading contributors that will virtually guarantee price resistance:

Selling Price: 80% of salespeople use price as a competitive weapon. Prospects rate price on a scale of 1 to 10 as a 2.5 and salespeople rate it as 8.0. Most salespeople aren't aware that the opening price gambits by prospects are always just a ploy. 95% of all purchase decisions are made on a non-price basis. On most surveys, price is generally the fourth or fifth consideration.

Lack of Self Esteem and Confidence: It really isn't so much believing in your product, as it is believing in yourself. Self-esteem and belief in your product or service generally go in tandem.

Needs based Selling: People don't buy what they need, they buy what they want. Needs based selling (understanding their specifications, applications, and requirements) marginalizes and commoditizes your offering because people rarely pay a premium for what they need. They always will pay a premium for what they want. This is a classic Chevrolet versus BMW motivation. Most of us need a car (Chevrolet) but want a BMW.

Lack of a Healthy Pipeline: Salespeople who sell out of desperation generally have a poor pipeline of prospects. Consistent prospecting can help you arm yourself to be more effective in price battles.

Need for Approval: Salespeople with a high need for approval will tend to find themselves vulnerable to price shoppers. Their need to be liked, validated or to avoid healthy confrontation will generally supersede their need to sell healthy margins.

Selling at the Wrong Level: The higher up the food chain you sell, the less likely price will be a dominant factor. Most senior level people, unlike purchasing agents, don't have the time or the inclination to do comparison shopping, because their mandate is more about growth, vision and profit.

The following are specific tactics, scripts, and verbiage to deal with price shoppers:

- *"I understand price is an important factor for you, and it should be. As you can imagine, we offer a full range of prices, dependent on many variables. At this stage, I'm not sure what is right for you. Can we first establish what you need and why you need it? Then I'll be more than happy to give you the price right down to the penny."*
- *"You say you can't afford it. I certainly can appreciate that. This isn't right for everyone. What, if anything, will you accept as proof that you can afford it?"*
- *"My product is one of the more premium services around... is that a reason for us to stop talking?"*
- *"The good news is, I can help you solve your problem. The bad news is, it will cost more than you anticipated."*
- *"You must have found a comparable product with high quality and service for less."*
- *"I'm going to ask you a tough question, and I hope you can appreciate why I'm asking this: Are you the least expensive company in town?"*
- *"Our customers basically fall into three categories. There are those fortunate few who elect to invest $300,00 on a long-term project. Then there are those who invest $200,000 for a medium-sized project; and then, those who invest $50,000 for a kickoff engagement to test the waters. Which best fits you?"*
- *"The common law of business prohibits paying a little and getting a lot."*
- *"Good things are seldom cheap. And cheap things are seldom good."*
- *"We are a little less than a lot and more than a little, is how our customers would typify us."*
- *"Are you concerned with price or total cost?"*

- *"Could you ever see yourself paying more for something you could get for less?"*
- *"Sometimes our product is expensive and it is a good deal, and sometimes it is expensive and it isn't a good deal. Let's see which is the case for you."*
- *"Would it ever be of concern that you paid less on the front end and more on the back end?"*
- *"Is price your only concern?"*
- *"It is very expensive if it doesn't work or if we aren't a good fit for you. Let's see if we are first a good fit."*
- *"Everyone is in a tight mode. Is this going to break the bank for you?"*
- *"Your company doesn't have deep pockets and short fingers, does it?"*
- *"If you can get it for less, then you should. You'd be fiscally irresponsible if you didn't. If I were in your shoes, I'd do the same. However, the only way you could possibly get burned is if you were not comparing apples to apples. Are you open to discussing that?"*
- *"I know price is important to you. So we can compare all variables, do you mind sharing with me what you are comparing us with, in concluding our price is high?"*
- *"Mr. Prospect, how are you evaluated and what will you be remembered for two years from now? That you got a good low price on the front end or that the project was a big success because you didn't cut any corners and you covered all your bases? A lower price just lowers your risk on price but not on quality."*
- *"Let's assume, all things being equal, even price, who are you most confident with at this stage?"*
- *"Are you concerned with price or cost? Price is the initial acquisition cost. Cost is the total ownership cost. It includes all the things after you've acquired the product. Are you open to discussing that to make a better comparison?"*
- *"I'm curious, how do you mean 'it costs too much'? Compared to what?"*

- *"Why do you feel you can't pay this price? I'd like to understand if I can."*
- *"If you think our prices are high, just wait until you see what it costs you when it is cheaper. Unless entry cost is your only concern?"*
- *"Let's assume price wasn't an issue for you. What else is holding you back?"*
- *"With all due respect, we are looking for customers who value getting more and therefore are willing to pay more, not people who can afford to pay less to get less."*
- *"You can pay a little more now or potentially pay a lot more later."*
- *"Would you agree on a practical level a product or service is worth what it can do for you and not what you paid for it?"*
- *"The most expensive doctor in the world can be is a cheap one."*
- *"Do you think anyone has the money for this?"*
- *"When you say I'm expensive, is that a question or just an observation?"*
- *"If you leave it up to me, I have very expensive taste and I'll recommend something that is very expensive. So can you share with me what you had in mind?"*
- *"Thank God our prices are high. And yet you are still talking with me. Why?"*
- *"Do you have any suspicions that easy money comes with a high price in this situation?"*
- *"When you say it is high, I'm assuming you will share with me if it is justified or not from your perspective?"*
- *"The price will be in direct proportion to how small or big your perceived problems are."*

19

To Find Problems, You Must Trigger Problems

The following are some of the problem prompters I use for my company. You will notice the questions are frequently framed in hypothetical language and there is an effort to bring balance to the questions. Questions hypothetically posed tend to be less direct and intimidating. Also, the questions generally have a strong emotional appeal as opposed to an ineffective rational appeal.

Some questions are formulated in a positive light to underscore the gap between what the prospect says is good and what a good situation truly looks like. You'll also notice that in some cases, there are multiple follow-up questions on the main problem points to go deeper in order to expose denial or to uncover problems that the prospect never thought they had. The idea is to be prepared to keep your prospect engaged and have enough ammo in your arsenal to follow up with deeper questions to dent your prospect's armor.

These problem prompter questions and statements are designed for scenarios where your prospect tells you they have no problems or no interest and you want to confirm or challenge that notion with thought-provoking questions to find or create problem. Here are some examples:

- *Are you running into challenges where your salespeople are all running around in many different directions without any unified sales strategy making it difficult to control, monitor and lead your sales team and making it difficult to predict and forecast revenue consistently?*

Do you help them manage their pipelines on deals they're closing?

Do they have the same criteria as you?

Do you have a systematic sales strategy and process that they can properly execute beyond order entry?

Do you have monthly strategy sessions beyond administrative and moaning sessions, where you review new industries, markets, and how to penetrate higher levels in organizations?

- *The sales group is a mystery. All the other departments are easier to hold accountable and manage but sales continues to lag behind the rest of the company.*

- *They don't know if they have the right people to get them to the next level. They aren't all hitting their numbers consistently, and they don't know who to change and who to upgrade.*

Do you use a commission based compensation program as your main management tool and then try to traffic manage your people?

It sounds like you have an active recruiting plan, where you are not held hostage to your salespeople.

You have a "no excuse" environment. You take total responsibility and you don't blame your salespeople for shortcomings.

- *At some point in your career you were the best salesperson and you moved into sales management where you've become a competent sales administrator. You manage information well, and do a good job of putting out fires, but don't do as good of a job challenging developing, motivating, counseling, coaching, and leading your people.*

It sounds like your people are very motivated and goal directed and focused.

I assume you have a defined sales plan which the salespeople help developed based on how much money they want to make, what their personal goals are, what revenue goals they are going to commit to and the activity needed to accomplish those goals?

I assume you actively hold them accountable?

Do you have a specific plan for new business generation and a separate plan for account development with existing accounts?

Do you know the percentage necessary for calls, quotes and closing rate?

Do you spend an average of 1 to 2 days in the field coaching your people each week?

In other words, you've got goals, they've got goals, and they are in sync?

- *It's been a tough last couple of years for most companies with the economy and most are starting to see things heating up again. But from a motivation perspective they are in a rut where they've been doing the same old things, the same old ways and expecting different results. Their sales team is lacking energy and innovation. Are you experiencing this?*

- *Do your people ever feel used and frustrated and out of control in the selling process where the prospect holds all the cards, calls all the shots, and it starts to affect their motivation, ultimately taking an emotional toll out of them and consequently de-motivating them?*

*They don't suffer call reluctance or inconsistency in performance... lots of peaks and valleys?

*Do they ever return from calls triumphantly, all enthusiastic and convinced they've made a sale, only to find out they were being used?

*Are they very good at qualifying accounts, knowing when to fold or hold?

*Are they very good at sizing up opportunities, where they know if they have live deals or not? Do they do their due diligence by finding out what problems the prospect has, the costs and consequences of those problems and their willingness to change? Do they know their prospect's budget, understand the decision making process and know the timing of the deal?

- *I sometimes hear complaints from owners like yourself who tell me their salespeople sell well only as long as the economy is strong, but suffer when there is any downturn. Is that a concern here at all?*

- *They're technically adept and very knowledgeable about your products, but do they too often get reduced to free consultants who aren't paid and rewarded for their ideas and efforts?*

- *Do your salespeople get beaten up on price where they're constantly cutting prices at the cost of lower margins and they're frequently battling differentiating themselves from their competition and trying to prevent commoditization?*

- *Their salespeople are doing well by default because the company is well positioned in the marketplace, the economy is improving, the company has an excellent reputation and product line that is the envy of the industry, good pricing, lots of leads that you pay for, and the salespeople have been in their territories for a long* time. *In other words, they are succeeding primarily because they are riding on the coattails of a successful company and they are not proportionately carrying their weight*

- *They are successful, but they are over relying on selling transactionally (onezies, twozies) at low margins. They aren't getting enough long term, strategic, profitable, major account business. They struggle selling high in their accounts and they don't sell deep, getting add on business.*

*You must have very strategic sellers that have healthy selling cycles and reasonably low costs of sales. You must have a healthy mix of business that covers your whole product or service offering, leaving very few holes in your sales strategy?

- *They are selling the wrong mixture of accounts. They are in a comfort zone and spend too much time on small accounts where they are liked, and aren't selling high in the organization where they can build longer-term relationships that are more profitable.*

- *They succeed at the expense of the company because they've been in the territory a long time. They have a few plum accounts that they rest their laurels on, but they aren't growing their account base and bringing in new business. They are gliding and retiring on the job and living off the fat of past successes at your expense.*

- *They are disproportionately successful because they rely on management to qualify their deals and help them close their big deals, consequently eating up a lot of management time and company resources, while at the same time, getting full credit and commission.*

- *They are excuse makers; always blaming the economy, competition, pricing, your products and not taking personal*

> *responsibility for their results and hence, are difficult to manage and lead.*

It's difficult to implement this selling process; you will probably experience a lot of problems and challenges yourself in learning it. However, this will result in even more empathy with your prospects.

20

Voice Mail: The Bane of Existence for Salespeople

Voice mail is the bane of existence for most salespeople. The reason salespeople don't get their unsolicited messages returned is because they look and sound like every other salesperson out there. Their messages are too company-centric and not enough customer-centric.

Salespeople also are their own worst enemies by reinforcing negative stereotypes of being obnoxiously upbeat and overly familiar, without offering any balance or neutrality to their approach.

To increase your percentages, leave messages that are thought-provoking and triggers doubt,insecurity, or a sense of impending risk. A guiding principle to all unsolicited voice mail messages that you should always employ is: don't tell them about how you can help them or what makes you different. Rather, tell them the problems you address and fix.

Keep in mind that prospects rightfully don't care about your company, your leadership positions, your storied history, or your state of the art technology. They care only about themselves and are predisposed to returning your call if you craft your message towards matters that cause them dissatisfaction and inconvenience.

For your messages to hit home, they should have an emotional appeal, instead of a typically dry logical and rational appeal. Your hope is to get a little under their skin by asking questions that create or find problems. You should leave your phone number but without requesting that your prospect expressly call you. This way, you sound interested buy not needy and anxious.

The following is an example of a voice mail marketing campaign that I did for my company that can be coordinated with corresponding letters, emails, and even faxes. You can take bits and pieces of this campaign and adapt it to a single message or have an abbreviated campaign of 3 or 4 calls. The frequency can be every week or every 3 days. You can also automate the process and leverage your time by leaving prerecorded messages at off-hours. For this campaign to work effectively, your tone should be neutral, unenthusiastic, relaxed and conversational. Your messages should be pain based, and to increase curiosity you may want to consider leaving out your company's name.

Message 1

"John, this is Rick Farrell calling and if you are like a lot of Presidents I talk to who are frustrated with their salespeople who are constantly getting beaten up on price where their margins are eroding and finding it is getting increasingly more difficult to differentiate themselves from their competition, then perhaps we should talk. I can be reached at 773-404-7915. Thanks!"

Message 2

"John, this is Rick Farrell calling again. I left you a message earlier this week about companies' frustrations with salespeople selling on price. Since I didn't hear back from you, I thought I'd bring up another frustration that companies are facing today. That is, their sales team's inability to qualify opportunities properly, resulting in a lot of expensive and wasteful quoting, proposing and bidding. If you are running into this, maybe we should talk. I can be reached at 773-404-7915. Thanks!"

Message 3

"John, this is Rick Farrell calling once again. You probably recognize my name by now. I've left you a couple of messages about underperforming salespeople. Since I haven't heard back from you on any of those issues, I thought I would change direction and talk about sales management concerns. If you are having frustrations with sales managers who aren't

holding salespeople accountable and sales are suffering because of that, then we should definitely talk this time. Again, I can be reached at 773-404-7915."

Message 4

"John, this is Rick Farrell calling once more. Hopefully you haven't grown too tired of my messages. Today's message will be brief. Do you find that your salespeople are running around in many different directions without a unified sales strategy, making it difficult to control, monitor, lead and predictably forecast revenue consistently? If so, I am at 773-404-7915."

Message 5

"John, this is Rick Farrell signing off with my last and final call. Do you ever have lingering doubts about whether you have the right people to grow your company to the next level? They aren't all hitting their numbers consistently and you don't know who to change and who to upgrade. My number one last time is 773-404-7915 if you are open to chat."

I have a client who has five salespeople who have prerecorded four messages that they use on an automated voice mail campaign that nets them quality leads every month with minimal effort and time. Whether you do a formal campaign or a one-time message, it is critical to sell problems and consequences and not your company, capabilities, and why you are different. Gear all your appeals to their problems.

21

You are Not in the Business of What You Sell

The most important information in the selling event is the information your prospect has. The prospect has all the answers and the seller has all the questions. Most salespeople believe they have all the answers and they come across as arrogant and uncaring. Arrogant based selling is built on the theory that if we sell it, they will buy it.

That is why the prospect is always the best salesperson at the selling event. Let the prospect tap their information to help you build your own business case. To effectively accomplish this you must take a non-attached and non-selling posture. We put foolish faith in what we know. Give your prospect the space to vocalize their issues.

When you come to the selling event with a beginner's mind, an empty vessel with nothing to prove, with a clean slate free of expectations, it allows you to honor and empower your prospect's ability to seek their own solutions, answer their own objections and create their own conclusions.

By sparingly using your information, you create curiosity and a desire to learn more. Also, you don't fall into the trap of being a fixer. And as women will attest, nothing will undermine your case quicker than being a fixer who is more intent on resolving a problem than one who wants to first understand it.

Intellectual capital isn't created so much by what you know about your products and solutions, but what you learn about your prospect's business, priorities, goals and critical success factors. Your product information and expertise only become valuable to your prospect when you use this knowledge as a conduit to uncover, discover and bring to the surface your prospect's problems in a unique and thought-provoking way. Only use your knowledge and information as a tool to gain and acquire more additional information. This way you allow your prospects to see their business in a way they have never seen or examined before. It is more important to know intimately the ins and outs of your prospect's business than it is to know the ins and outs of your own product line. The old adage that the truth will set you free is relevant in relation to information. Work hard to get the truth (the right information). Most salespeople avoid the truth like the plague.

A new mindset to manage information is to believe that you are no longer in the business of what you sell. Being in the business of what you sell always puts the emphasis on the wrong party -- you. You are actually in the business of understanding your prospect's business regardless of what you sell. Software companies are major offenders of this tenet. Because they believe they are in the technology sector, they put all the emphasis on the latest and greatest technology advancements and breakthroughs, bypassing the prospect's business, their needs and critical success factors.

If your product or service has a rich and colorful product heritage, it may be initially difficult for you to reposition your mindset to stop thinking about your product or service as something that simply goes into your prospect's business. Whether we know it or not, we all sell intangibles. Nothing, including physical hard goods, is anything but an idea on how to add profit or lower cost to your prospect's business.

Moreover, prospects don't evaluate your offerings in a vacuum. The big area that salespeople fail to gather information on is in relation to other investments they are evaluating, in other totally different areas of their business. Many times your biggest competition is the prospect investing their resources or re-channeling their budget to a totally different area in their business.

By helping your prospects look at their entire business in respect to your offering, you help them independently arrive at their own conclusions as to where they can get the greatest return on their time, their money and their resources. You develop a business case based on all the variables in their business.

Companies are quickly realizing that they are only as good as the salespeople who represent them. Because of product and service parity, companies can no longer expect sustained competitive advantages from their products or service offerings to carry the day.

Too often, the more information the prospect has, the greater the resistance and the longer your sales cycle will be. View your information as intellectual capital that has high value and needs to be protected and strategically allotted when the timing is appropriate.

You don't want to just get information for the sake of information. The best information that you can get is information that leads you to the truth. This will require you to ask tough questions and to have a very high level of trust and rapport with your prospect. Always be diligent in believing that you don't have a corner on the market when it comes to the truth about your sales proposition and sales offering. Truth isn't exclusive. It belongs to all of us equally. What is truthful to one person isn't truthful to another. Exclusive concepts of truth are delusional. It is very hard for salespeople to find the truth of a situation because they don't take a balanced perspective about another's own unique version of their truth. Salespeople generally are too vigilant in believing their own B.S.

22

The Myth of the Self-Initiated Motivated Salesperson

Most small to midsize companies I work with don't have a sales plan. Most mistakenly believe that salespeople are internally motivated and directed where it is unnecessary or over-kill. When a sales organization has 100% commission salespeople, it fails to put together a sales plan because it doesn't believe it can control or influence an independent sales force.

The biggest reason sales organizations don't take the time or the effort to do a sales plan is because it is time-consuming on the front end and time-consuming on the back end. It takes real commitment and a disciplined approach to put together an effective plan.

Because of the personal nature of a sales plan, such as aspirations, income targets and lifestyle goals, most managers are not accustomed to or comfortable digging deep into the heads of their salespeople. They don't realize that emotions are some of the key drivers of salespeople.

Most companies have a loosely knit sales figure to aim for, but generally they don't go beyond that. A good sales plan is enforceable and holds salespeople accountable. Too many companies fear a defined sales plan because they will have to face the stark reality that they have some non-performing salespeople who are costing them money and they are not willing to act on it.

If they did act on it, they would have to play the enforcer role and they would rather spend the extra money (income, benefits) to let it slide and hope that the salesperson will leave on their own or they will naturally correct themselves through their own devices.

Managing salespeople can be a thankless job. That is why there are few talented sales managers. Companies too often mistakenly take their best salesperson out of the field and make them sales managers. This often falls short because of the lack of experience of the sales manager.

Another major reason that sales plans are not instituted or properly executed is because once you see the writing on the wall for certain underperforming salespeople, you need to start recruiting and hiring again. Companies have an attitude that the devil you know is better than the devil you don't know.

Now that you know some of the real reasons companies don't use sales plans, let's look at the internal dynamics of what makes up a sales plan.

The three major parts are:

1. Personal Goal Setting
2. Formalized Sales Plan
3. Monthly Reinforcement and Accountability

Accurate forecasting coupled with a well thought-out and detailed sales plan can help companies avoid problems, anticipate problems, plan for growth, identify new markets, and provide direction for its salespeople. It also can help manage staff, production, and cash flow needs more effectively. Although it requires an upfront investment of time and effort, it ultimately will help companies spend more time creating their business rather than reacting and constantly putting out fires.

A good sales plan works to improve shortcomings in the past and capitalize on growth opportunities for the future. It gets your salespeople to focus their attention on growing their major accounts, spend less time on non-productive activity and focus on how they can grow new accounts. Once accomplished, it is easier for management to lead, manage, track and make tough decisions on better data.

STEP 1 Personal Goal Setting of Salespeople

One key characteristic of high performing salespeople is they have written goals which have a goal date, and those are monitored and changed annually. Because salespeople come to work each day for their own reasons and not for management's reasons, personal goal setting is the hallmark of a successful sales plan. Salespeople are competitive by nature and having them focus on their personal goals and using their career to help them achieve these goals can only help them to be more focused and motivated. Once they home in on all income goals and materialistic goals, they can use this as their own personal benchmark for their professional revenue goals and activity goals.

The following are some of the more obvious areas that should be considered for a complete goal package:

1. Materialistic Goals: What new possessions do you want?
2. Vacation Goals: What destinations?
3. Retirement Goals: When, where and how much?
4. Professional Goals: What can you do to enhance your profession?
5. Career Goals: How far, how high and with whom?
6. Hobby Goals: If you had the time and money, what would you like to do?
7. Personal Goals: What is important to you to do with your life, spirituality and with your family?
8. Knowledge Goals: Professionally and personally
9. Money Goals: How much? What are your 5, 10, 15, and 20-year plans?
10. Health and Beauty goals: How do you plan to stay healthy?

To make things easy, each goal has a stated mission, a due date and a specific plan. Some goals will have a few objectives and others will have many.

STEP 2 Formalized Sales Plan

Depending on your benchmarks, a sales plan should have an overview for each salesperson and their territory or account base, followed by a specific account analysis.

The overview should include threats, opportunities, present situation, competitive analysis, and trends.

The account analysis should include two major categories: existing accounts and new business. Within each category there should be a breakdown of A/B/C accounts. Information should be exact and to the point. "Less is more" is a good standard.

The following are suggestions for the account analysis:

1. Last year's volume
2. Market share or total opportunity
3. Sales projection
4. Key contacts
5. Number of sales calls made last year to that account
6. Number of sales calls projected for this year to that account
7. Type of account (A/B/C)
8. Goals, strategies and plans for this account

The key for management is to locate where salespeople are wasting their time, spending too much time or too little time, calling too high or too low, existing business/new business ratios, and validity of overall sales strategy.

STEP 3 Monthly Reinforcement and Accountability

It is recommended that you review bi-annually and annually your sales plan with your salespeople. Review the key benchmarks as to where they are, year to date, and what revisions and changes they have to make to be on target with their goals. This should be done on a one-on-one basis.

Most sales organizations, when they do sales meetings, will run them anytime from weekly, monthly, or quarterly meetings. Unfortunately the meetings are bull sessions, product updates or just internal reporting. There is not enough time spent on accountability and helping the salespeople manage their activity, accounts, and goals.

The most important exercise a manager can do with their group is monthly pipeline reviews. This status report has each salesperson detailing their immediate and long-term deals that make up their active pipeline of deals. Effective managers have a defined systematic process to use that is not arbitrary and does not just ask, *"Where are you with your goals this month?"*

The key elements cover the main revenue benchmarks that the salesperson has committed to. Typically they are monthly or weekly activity (dials, people reached, appointments, quotes, referrals and sales) and an outlined progress report for all the deals they are forecasting in their pipeline.

The progress report or forecast will differ for every company because everyone has different benchmarks or priorities to measure. The following is a description of some of the key elements to track in the sales process:

1. Motive for change: What are the customer's problems, what are the costs and what is the tolerance for change?
2. Investment: Is the customer willing to invest time, resources, and money to address their problem? What is the timing for change?
3. Decision process: The who, what, where, when, why and how. What are the steps for change and timetable for each step?
4. Solution: When and what will be the solution?
5. Closure: What is the timing for a decision?

Some companies might have more steps. The point is to at least include the preceding which will be universal for just about all sales situations. As you take your salespeople through each of these steps, you no longer have to rely on forecasting information like, *"They really like me, and I'm their guy. I know they have the money and I'm confident we have this one."* It is not a bad idea to assign a percentage for each step or define the key benchmarks in the sales process.

Management can now be very clear for each account the salesperson is forecasting as to where they are, what they have done right, what they have done improperly, what they need to do next, what is the percentage of closure and what can the salesperson do to repeat or prevent what they have done so far for the future.

23

Time is Enemy Number One

Ever-shortening product life cycles due to rapid technological advancements in the global economy are causing virtually every product and service to quickly become a commodity. Given the warp speed economy in which we do business, nothing is more important in salespeople's work life than time.

Time is your single most important leverage. Unfortunately it is a depreciating asset that is non-recoverable. Once you've given it away, you can never get it back. Since time is money, you should be discriminating as to whom, when and under what circumstances you should allocate it. Not only do we have to manage spending time on the right people, we also have to work to shorten the length of time it takes to sell people. Equally important is the time it takes to lose deals. Bad news is good news when it's received early. Too often salespeople operate under the belief that "my time isn't as valuable as yours". They would rather patiently wait for the occasional bones or crumbs that prospects throw their way than going out and looking for better opportunities. Clients receive this unintended message and they have no problem having you go on unending fool's errands. Many salespeople would rather chase opportunities in the face of insurmountable odds and face inevitable failure than to prospect. A lot of misdirected use of time is simply avoidance activity. There will always be more opportunities to invest in than there is time and resources. Therefore, salespeople should be discriminatory and selective with their time.

Traditional salespeople operate under a false sense of security that if they persist, outlast the competition, show the customer they care, and be assertive, they will ultimately prevail. In reality, this is simply not true. Professional salespeople are good at qualifying their opportunities and cutting their losses when they are operating under non-optimum conditions. They know there are only two winners in a competitive selling situation: the salesperson who was awarded the deal and the salesperson who lost early and saved time.

In today's marketplace selling is more about sifting, sorting and selecting opportunities that have the greatest likelihood of closing, as opposed to always trying to sell, convince, persuade and cajole. Salespeople who take on a business owner mentality look at acquisition cost as overhead that needs to be judiciously guarded and protected. Unfortunately, 80% of what salespeople are spending their time on has a low value. Working in this way is a waste of your most valuable asset, time, and not consistent with a business owner mentality.

Time should also be viewed as an inventory control system. A business owner who looks at inventory has one thing in mind: turn it as quickly as possible, because time is money. A salesperson with a business owner mentality sees their sales pipeline in the same way. A poor inventory control system in sales is a surplus in the pipeline of accounts that aren't viable, closable, and moving in a timely fashion. Time-oriented salespeople know the longer it takes to sell prospects, the more time and money they have to invest elsewhere.

In sales, you only have a limited amount of sales calls you can make in a year. They represent your acquisition or opportunity cost. Hence, sales calls are your currency. Where you invest them will determine your return. It is important for salespeople to create rules of engagement: what is the minimum acceptable action I will accept from a prospect? If you aren't getting results in exchange for your effort, you are wasting your time and your money.

Unlike relationship selling where you don't have to continue reselling a customer when you get an order, transactional selling can be very time consuming and costly. In transactional selling you incur the direct costs of selling your customer over and over again each time they present you with an opportunity until the sale is made or lost. While you are waiting to close one customer, your time is delayed in pursuing any new opportunities. This is relevant also in the opportunity costs of sending information, doing presentations, filling out quotes and following up with disinterested prospects.

The name of the game in sales is efficiency. But the process most salespeople use is appallingly inefficient. They waste an untold amount of their time. Frequently, they allocate their time equally among the entire universe of opportunities and wait until prospects disqualify themselves. They aren't treating their time with respect and it shouldn't come as a shock that their prospects don't either. The more you respect your time, the more likely you will attract prospects who will treat you and your time with the same respect.

In the old days you could use dogged determination as an effective sales strategy. Salespeople would simply employ a full frontal assault and mercilessly chase prospects down until the prospect said, *"Never call me again,"* or they threw up the white flag and said, *"Enough is enough, I'll buy."* But with the advent of do not call lists, voice mail and email coupled with hectic work schedules, long work hours, less loyalty with suppliers and more bottom line accountability, this bygone strategy no longer works. Salespeople can no longer be world-class acrobats, jumping through hoops and using false hope as a sales strategy.

Salespeople also fall into the trap of spending too much time with the wrong type of opportunities and not enough time with the right opportunities. These are the type of salespeople who have the exact opposite problem that most salespeople have who wantonly and indiscriminately call on everyone. They are very good at precisely targeting key accounts in segments where they aren't competitive or it is a poor match. It is fondly called the Mt. Everest effect because it is there and it is monumentally huge. They go after big-name accounts which they don't have a chance in the world to get.

Another common mistake salespeople have about time is that they believe they can manage it. Time management is an oxymoron. You can't manage time, only what you do with time. In essence you must become a master of prioritizing. Most salespeople make the mistake of trying to manage time by organizing their week with activity that is unqualified and a poor use of their time. If one looked at their calendar they would be impressed with their organizational skills but upon further examination, they would see they have organized and arranged their week with sales calls that will at best only net them a 5-10% return. There will always be more opportunities to invest in than there is time. Therefore, one of the greatest skill sets a salesperson can have is being able to quickly assess whether a prospect has a "compelling reason to change", and being able to confidently walk away from opportunities that will be a time drain.

Time is money and salespeople need to be fiscally responsible. Peter Drucker wrote in *The Effective Executive* that one needs to know what to do with their time and what not to do. This is the power of being discriminatory. The sign of a good salesperson is to know which business to pursue. The sign of a truly accomplished salesperson is knowing what not to pursue and when to cut their losses. A recent study commissioned by *Fortune Magazine* concluded that a leading indication of executive denial is a background in sales. The conclusion is that hope and reckless determination are not a stable strategy in today's marketplace.

The customers with whom you do business always pay for those with whom you do not. Your mandate is to maximize your time with those prospects which you have the highest likelihood to do business with and minimize your time with those who have a low likelihood of doing business with you. Protecting and guarding your time lowers your costs of sales.

Effective salespeople are like money managers or portfolio managers. Windows of opportunity come and go so quickly that you always have to alter your portfolio. You ruthlessly replace the old and inefficient with the new. This strategy is effective for both parties because when you and the prospect don't waste each other's time everyone wins. If your time isn't being respected or it isn't being reciprocated, know that it may be time to exit.

As you think of yourself as a money manager, you start to think of your time as an investment account. You are either investing in it wisely or wastefully withdrawing from it. If you earn $150,000 and waste an hour each day, that is $18,750 you are wasting and withdrawing. Big prospects justify major time and small prospects justify small amounts of time.

If time management is critical to one's success, timing is even more important. With whom and under what circumstances are critical elements of timing. Good timing will carry the day more so than a superior offering. Therefore, time your offerings when your prospect is in a position to make decisions that can forward your cause. In real estate it is location, location and location. In sales it is timing, timing and timing.

24

The Commodity Slide

All products and services, from the day they hit the market, slide predictably to commodity status, from high price/high profit to low price/low profit. This happens as a function of their product passing naturally through the four stages of its life cycle.

There are different selling methodologies that also tend to follow the commodity slide through its natural stages. Ironically, many salespeople don't adjust and adapt their selling strategies to the four stages. They continue to sell a commodity as if it were still unique and distinguishable. The commodity slide also holds a great lesson for your sales proposals and information. The longer your proposal and solution sit out there, with time, the faster it loses its value and its ability to withhold price pressures. The passing of time eventually marginalizes all products and in relation to your proposals and information: time kills all deals. However, many salespeople operate under an entirely different reality. They believe the longer their deals hang out there, the longer they have to endear themselves to their prospect and outlast and outflank their competition with their dogged determination.

The following are descriptions of the four stages of the commodity slide in how it relates to your selling strategy and how you position your product and service:

Stage 1

An interesting example of the commodity slide that typifies the four stages is FedEx. Fred Smith, its founder, was an MBA student at Harvard

Business School and did a paper on a transportation scheme he had for the logistic market based on a hub and spoke business model. His professor, deeming the paper interesting but impractical, gave it a C. Fred Smith, in the classic rebellious nature of an entrepreneur, dropped out of school and borrowed some money from friends and family to execute his innovative idea. In the early days, the joke around the company was there were more planes than packages on some days. However, as luck may have it, one day Fred was golfing with some buddies and one of their guests was from a staffing company. After hearing Fred bemoan the costly challenges of having to fully staff his operation for peak packaging activity, the owner of the staffing company knew he could save Fred millions of dollars by cutting his payroll and staffing his operation with flexible part-time workers who could be called upon on short notice to handle the peaks and valleys of FedEx's volume. At this stage, did Fred Smith quibble with price? Absolutely not. He was delighted to be saving millions. In Stage 1, the predominate selling methodology is customer fulfillment. Any salesman with a shoeshine and a smile can sell at this stage. Salespeople are simply glorified order takers. Motivated buyers who have not had the luxury of time and resources to shop for your proposal characterize sales proposals at this stage. Stage 1 is also typified by high demand and low supply, allowing sales to be easy and profitable. The question for the customer at Stage 1 is not even *"which one should I buy?"*, since there is no competition. Rather, the concern is, *"how fast I can get it?"* Costs are high. Sellers are in control and have all the power.

Stage 2

As Fred Smith's company matured, he brought on professional managers to run his different departments. One of his first hires was in the area of human resources. The new head, who had had previous relationships with other staffing firms, opened up the competition for their staffing requirements. Since the incumbent realized the selling situation was heating up as the onslaught of competitors started knocking on FedEx's door, the incumbent realized that they would have to start differentiating their offering by adding value or different features and benefits to maintain their competitive advantage. They also had to sharpen their pencil on price in Stage 2 since the buyer has more options. The focus moved from *"how do I get it?"* to *"which product offers the most value?"*. Unlike Stage 1, where the customer is solely focused on their problem, Stage 2 represents a subtle, but important shift to additional and enhanced choices that are available to them. The focus was now more on the product and less on the problem. This is where salespeople became value sellers or feature and benefit sellers to differentiate themselves and to underscore their value. Your sales proposals in Stage 2 have the vulnerability to be shopped for the first time. Therefore, timing of information becomes more important.

Stage 3

Stage 3 is personified by supply equaling or exceeding demand. There is an overabundance of "me too" products that are barely distinguishable from one another. The product is now a true commodity. However, most salespeople are conditioned to think otherwise and continue to sell distinguishing characteristics that no longer are unique. Price is now the driving factor and customers now no longer ask, *"How do I get one?"* (Stage 1), or *"Which is the best?"* (Stage 2), they now ask *"How can I get it for the cheapest price?"* (Stage 3). Now the original problem the prospect had is so far removed from their awareness that it is more difficult for salespeople to be problem solvers. Prospects can now hoodwink salespeople into believing they are no different than the competition. Prospects can now cover up and gloss over the original problem that initially compelled them to seek a solution. At this stage your information and unique proposals are all but neutralized. Proposals sit out there longer since the prospect isn't as focused on their original problem and proposals lose their potency and value. Once again, time kills all deals. The longer they sit out there, the greater the likelihood they will go south. Ten to fifteen years ago, as a lot of products were entering Stage 2, companies staged a comeback to combat their commoditization. They came up with the idea of customer service as a truly distinguishable and bankable differentiator. But time eroded that selling fad because everyone jumped on the same bandwagon and eventually started to look and sound like everyone else. Salespeople started to sing from the value-added hymnbooks and they got some decent traction out of it but eventually it started to sing hollow.

Stage 4

To combat these new economic realities, a small select group of companies have entered a stage, for lack of a better name, called Stage 4. They now distinguish themselves solely on how they sell and engage their prospect. They know this is a limited window of opportunity to get a leg up on the competition by repositioning themselves as problem solvers and change agents. This is truly the last bastion of differentiation available to them. They know that the salesperson who does the best job of identifying, isolating and understanding their prospect's problems will consistently outsell competitors who have price advantages and superior solutions. People still buy from people they like, but what is so important in this last stage is, people buy from people they believe have the patience, expertise, and industry knowledge to understand their unique problems and uncover business problems they never knew about.

Companies have adjusted their operations, their manufacturing and their cost structures quite well over the years to combat the inevitable slide their products and services experience. However, the one area that they have not adjusted to is how they reposition their offering to make up for the commoditization and marginalization of how they personally sell their products and services. Most sales organizations have salespeople who are experts at a game that is no longer being played. They continue to rely on antiquated and obsolete sales methodologies that no longer work in this ultra-competitive new information economy.

25

The Audacity of Hope: "Just Do It" Works
for Nike but is Fatal for Salespeople

Most salespeople, as a matter of habit and conditioning, still try to do business normally in a world that is anything but. There is a huge gap between today's selling strategies and today's market conditions. Salespeople in general ardently reject traditional selling in principle and embrace consultative selling, but have no real process to execute it with. A lot of apparent changes are merely window dressing. Salespeople are quickly finding out the hard way that identifying prospects' needs and giving solutions isn't consultative selling.

Salespeople need a better sales strategy and sales model. Imagine a quarterback coming out on the field during the last drive of the game, going into the huddle and enthusiastically saying to the players, "I don't know, let's just do it!" It works fine for Nike, but not for salespeople.

Manufacturers don't put up with line workers running production lines as they see fit. The administrative staff isn't allowed to run whatever software it is comfortable with. Companies allow certain things to happen in the sales department which they wouldn't permit anywhere else in the organization. Too many sales organizations believe that selling is a mystery, an afterthought and an ugly stepchild. Selling is truly the last frontier as far as efficiency is concerned. The process salespeople use has generally been unchanged for decades. The only meaningful changes in the sales department have been external. Sales departments have made large gains in mechanization, processing and tracking of orders and monitoring activity at the exclusion of creating a disciplined and systematic sales process. The easy answer to why is, because it is easier to change external processes than it is to change human behavior and interaction. Many companies have spent more money, time and resources on training clerical and factory workers than they have on their salespeople.

An effective sales process, vision, and disciplined strategy are the most important things a company can do for their sales effort. A systematic sales process can be a huge competitive advantage for a company. Salespeople can no longer fly by the seat of their pants with a "wing and a prayer" strategy, and expect to be productive and efficient anymore.

Salespeople need a documented and systematic process of predictable and repeatable steps that when followed consistently lead to a high percentage of success. Salespeople need to reinvent themselves and use a system that tells them in advance about whether they are winning, losing, what red flags to look for, how to change when needed and how to avoid similar missteps in the future. They need a system that puts them in control more and leads to uniform steps of action to produce specific outcomes.

Most selling is due to random events leading to accidents, both positive and negative. Salespeople instead need to lead prospects through sequential stages with a series of progressive, small commitments. *"Once salespeople adopt a universal system of problem solving, managing information and change, they can begin objectively to look at everything they do as an opportunity cost,"* says Jim Holden. They can better decipher and analyze their prospect's critical business issues to better determine if they have a compelling reason to change, what their problems are, how much it is costing them, what the decision process is, how much money is available, how change happens and what the competing priorities are.

Once salespeople have an end-to-end process that is sequentially linked and has stopgaps, they can optimize their time and resources more effectively and neutralize, contain, and counter-balance the prospect's superior buying process. This process of checks and balances utilizes universal questions to understand the process of change that prospects must go through and can be adapted to any type of personality a salesperson may have.

Salespeople tend to be very predictable and transparent. Their process is easily anticipated and neutralized by most sophisticated prospects. Most salespeople try to win the hearts and minds of their prospects by being energetic, confident and passionate in their pursuit. Instead they should be a resource, a leader and a change agent who helps the prospect in a sequential process that determines the cost of change and the will to follow through with it.

By following a defined sales stategy, you allow the prospect the opportunity to disqualify themselves each step along the way early and often, from beginning to end. By doing so, you start to sell consequences, problems and change, not products and solutions.

As you start to adapt this end-to-end process, you'll find that understanding is far more critical than persistence and giving out information.

Any disciplined sales process is typified by give and take. However, if salespeople or prospects are only taking, then there is no mutual basis for a relationship. It must be a mutual exploration and discovery process. To do so, you must be willing to suspend your ego, your expertise and all your hard-won product knowledge. You must learn to try to have unconditional acceptance of your prospect's point of view, regardless of whether it is wrong or not. You must learn to use your product expertise as a tool to get more information, not give away more information.

26

Hire Slow, Fire Fast

Hiring an effective salesperson is probably one of the most difficult hiring tasks in corporate America. Most managers err on talking too much about the company and not asking the tough questions to determine if a candidate can sell and more importantly, will they sell. Since salespeople are usually charming and persuasive, they frequently do their best selling at the interview and it goes down from there. And when times get tough they can be very persuasive in selling management on the health of their pipeline to buy themselves 3 to 6 more months in salary. In today's marketplace the classic selling skills that the majority of companies use in selecting salespeople are grossly obsolete and ineffective. Skills like being upbeat and optimistic, a warm and personable personality, dogged determination and persistence, a friendly and a talkative disposition, eagerness to please and to serve are characteristics that no longer ensure success, and quite often are characteristics that will predict mediocrity in the field.

One thing that definitely hasn't changed in determining the fate of a candidate is that they still must have a passion for success, and it greatly helps to be money motivated. They must be goal-oriented, have a strong self-concept, feel good about themselves and their company, and have a commitment to do whatever it takes to be successful.

Today's market demands a totally different type of salesperson. Characteristics like low need for approval, decisive decision making, advanced questioning and listening skills, and a high money threshold are the skill sets that will predict success.

These leading success indicators are rarely examined or closely exposed. They will be instrumental in predicting a fast ramp up time, an ability to walk away from unrealistic opportunities, healthy closing ratios, holding margins and effectively translating value, understanding the compelling reasons that would motivate someone to change or not, shorter selling cycles and the ability to build relationships and understanding.

The five key characteristics and predictors of performance are Buy Cycle, Need for Approval, Controlling Emotions, Money Concept, and Sales Beliefs.

BUY CYCLE

The way you buy is the way you'll sell. If you diligently do your research before an important major purchase, where you methodically take your time, patiently explore all of your options, gather volumes of information, and wait until the last moment to commit, you will always be vulnerable to prospects who buy the same way. Like attracts like, and this protracted style of buying can prove detrimental to a salesperson's ability to be productive. Long sales cycles can contribute to countless months of faithful follow-up on unqualified prospects who have no intent to buy. Salespeople with long buy cycles tend to have an over-evolved need for information. Hence when they are in a selling situation, they will tend to overwhelm and over-educate prospects with product information as opposed to relying on refined questioning and listening skills. They will become vulnerable to being unpaid consultants.

Because salespeople who have long buy cycles tend to overly "think things over" in their own personal purchasing patterns, they will attract prospects who are also indecisive in their decision making. This promotes allowing pull-backs, put-offs and procrastination and will have a direct impact on poor closing ratios. To expose these negative characteristics, ask candidates about their last major purchase and what the buying process was.

NEED FOR APPROVAL

The classic portrayal of a salesperson who companies look for is someone who is very enthusiastic and friendly, wants people to like them, is persuasive and talkative, intelligent and persistent. The problem is, most salespeople have taken this art form to an extreme. They aren't willing to challenge prospects and risk losing approval. They avoid asking tough questions that will get them the truth. They shy away from healthy confrontation and getting their own needs met as opposed to getting the more important need of making the sale. They are more concerned that prospects like them rather than respect them. These types are constantly used by their prospects for their expertise and solutions. Clarify this by asking sales candidates how they challenge prospects, how they ask tough questions, how they determine the viability of their opportunities and how they determine if they are wasting their time.

CONTROLLING EMOTIONS

Salespeople who effectively control their emotions sell like a change agent. They take a non-selling posture, ask questions that are unbiased and neutral, aren't afraid to hear "no" (they actually encourage it in some cases), and are in the moment where they can listen intently for what is being said and more importantly, what isn't being said. They sell from a position of a business strategist who gathers information to build a business case as opposed to building a product case. They have a quiet confidence instead of an excitable overly-emotional posture; they are more concerned with understanding than convincing; and they allow the prospect to self-discover the prospect's own conclusions without pushing their own agenda. They aren't emotionally involved in the outcome, so they minimize all the typical static of self-talk: "I wonder when they'll make up their mind; what if I don't make this sale; what am I going to spend my commission check on; and what am I going to do if they want to think it over?". Find out from sales candidates what their sales strategy is when they go into a sales call. More than likely, if they don't have a systematic sales methodology, they will tend to be needy, salesy, emotionally involved and out of control.

MONEY CONCEPT

Birds of a feather flock together. Salespeople who are price shoppers and comparison shoppers in their personal buying patterns will attract like-minded clients. Moreover, their personal concept of money and their comfort about talking about it openly will dramatically impact their ability to ask questions of their prospects about budgets and how they intend to fund their purchase. If a salesperson grew up in a household where the topic of money was taboo and the discussion of how much the neighbors paid for their new starter mansion was considered in bad taste, more then likely this will have a negative impact on that salesperson's ability to have an open dialogue with their prospects about their ability and their means to pay for their services. The irony is that the characteristics that make for a good neighbor are the same beliefs that could prove disastrous to a sales career.

Be aware of how the sales candidate handles the salary negotiation and if they hold their ground. Ask them how they determine budgets with their prospects. Find out what their personal concept of value is when they shop. If they are a bottom feeder and you sell a service that is a premium, then this could be a real red flag with this candidate's ability to hold margins.

COMPILED SALES BELIEFS

These are general sales beliefs that salespeople have that can negatively affect their performance on the job. The following are some of the more negative beliefs:

- It is important to educate my prospects.
- Prospects are honest.
- A good salesperson never gives up.
- It's okay if my prospect thinks it over, they will eventually buy from me.
- It's okay if my prospect shops around.
- A good salesperson does what the prospect tells them to do.
- Sending product information can forward the sale.

- All I need to do is to understand my prospect's requirements and specifications to make the sale.
- Any lack of results is due to the marketplace and the economy.
- I have to call on purchasing agents before I can call on decision makers.
- I don't need a sales process to be successful.
- Prospecting is a necessary evil.
- A good presentation is what makes the sale.

Make sure you ask sales candidates questions that will make them describe their sales process step by step. Ask behavioral question that will expose their weakness in asking questions and prematurely giving out information that makes them lose control in the sales process.

In summary, the hiring process should be a stringent process to weed out and try to expose sales weaknesses that will ultimately cause salespeople to be non-productive and ineffective. To avoid costly hiring problems we always advise our clients to hire slow and fire fast. Many companies use the interview predominantly to measure, chemistry, likeability, general sales experience, suitability of past experience and company and cultural fit. They so often fail in really determining if this candidate can sell, and, more importantly, will they sell? Do they have commitment, desire, and passion? Do they have what it takes to maintain margins, establish strong relationships that are built on trust and business strategy? Will they have healthy sales cycle, can they translate value instead of price, and can the candidate qualify and disqualify opportunities without wasting time? Since these skill sets are difficult to determine, we recommend that hiring managers use sales assessment tools to supplement their own findings from the interview process.

27

How to Lose Quickly, Effortlessly and with Minimal Time and Expense

If you find yourself prospecting and you run into intractable, deeply entrenched negative prospects, usually your best tactic is to take them to ground zero. Ground zero is the place of "no return" and is your last-ditch effort. The problem with stubborn prospects is the more you persist with them the stronger they will resist you.

If you are getting stonewalled after many futile attempts to engage them, then it makes sense to cut your losses and get one final confirmation that you are going nowhere quickly. This helps you maintain your dignity and helps eliminate any nagging doubts that they can be converted. Keep in mind, the best-case scenario usually for taking someone to ground zero is you don't continue to waste any more of your valuable time and energy chasing a phantom prospect.

Because the following questions and statements are fairly loaded, make sure you ask them in as non-threatening and graceful a manner as possible. Also be prepared for the worst; a quick and definitive negative response from your prospect.

- *"Has your company made the decision not to look at any other alternatives?"*
- *"Can I ask you a silly question? Do you believe that what you've got, within reason, is as good as it gets and doesn't get any better?"*
- *"Can I ask you a loaded question? If there was a better and more efficient way out there to improve your results, and I'm*

not sure if we even have it or not, are you even open to taking the time to look at it?"

- *"Are you at all open to extending me the professional courtesy of a few minutes of your time to discuss any possible shortfalls or issues in your organization?"*

- *"Is it the case that you don't have any problems or is it you don't have any problems that are worth your time discussing with me?"*

- *"Well, you certainly can't argue with success. However, what if you have some of these issues but you aren't even aware of them? It's the classic four-wall syndrome. You're too close or too accustomed to your problems that they no longer register. Or so long as you don't hear about them they aren't meaningful."*

- *"I may be pushing my luck, but it sounds like you have these problems but they are manageable or tolerable and you can live with them quite well. Don't fix it if it isn't really broke."*

- *"I assume you don't owe it to yourself or your company to further investigate issues that aren't perceived as a priority for you?"*

- *"Have you reached the conclusion that you have everything to gain and nothing to lose by staying with what you have and what you know?"*

- *"At this stage of the game have you concluded that what you don't know can't hurt you?"*

- *"Are you in that enviable position that we all seek, where your success is assured by your present course, you don't have to look over your shoulder, and constantly push the envelope to improve?"*

- *"Have you decided beyond a reasonable doubt that it isn't in your best interests to take any time or resources to explore other options?"*

- *"I assume there is no question that what got you to be successful today is the same that will allow you to be successful in the future?"*

The following questions and statements are not as forceful and definitive but can be very effective with prospects who love to talk and are always projecting optimism. These are the type of prospects who aren't forward thinking, objective and willing to emotionally step aside and take a constructive look at their problems. Instead of resisting them, use the following questions and statements as a way to nudge them. Overly optimistic prospects may not be willing to admit problems, but they may be willing to admit imperfections.

- *"I can see where that would make your life very easy."*
- *"You certainly are in an enviable position."*
- *"You certainly can't argue with success."*
- *"That must make your job very secure and fulfilling."*
- *"I can see why you would have no motivation to change."*
- *"It must be very gratifying to be in that ideal position."*
- *"You must consider yourself very lucky."*
- *"That must give you a lot of job security."*
- *"Sounds like smooth sailing at XYZ Company for you."*
- *"You certainly, for the time being, have a lot to be grateful for."*

Keep in mind that selling often has more to do with picking your battles wisely and cutting your losses than it does with asserting your will and trying to convert intractable prospects. Going to ground zero will more often than not save you time and energy but won't result often in forwarding your cause and moving you positively forward. This time saving strategy will also allow you to achieve closure on prospects who aren't open-minded, therefore minimizing lingering doubts about their feasibility. In sales there are always two winners. The first winner is the salesperson who was awarded the deal. The second winner is the salesperson who lost quickly, effortlessly and with minimum expenditure of valuable resources.

28

The Power of Suggestion

It is human nature for prospects to initially dismiss your selling points. However, you will find that any point you want to drive home, when referred to a third party, will have a better chance that your prospect will not dismiss it. Prospects are more apt to trust someone else's opinion, even if it is the exact one you are promoting, when you credit an outside source for the origination of an idea.

This is especially true with points of contention that are emotionally charged. By using a third party reference, you can test the waters for your ideas and be somewhat protected if it backfires. For example: *"We had a customer who complained about XYZ Corp in their ability to deliver on time. I don't suppose you have experienced poor delivery?"* And if you get a negative response you can fall back with, *"I didn't think so."* This allows you to minimize the disruption in the flow and momentum of your conversation.

Any time you can depersonalize your own selling points, you are perceived as less aggressive and generally more believable because you give your prospect the autonomy to self-discover their own conclusions. The power of suggestion can be effective and disarming. Moreover, third party references to problems that your prospect is experiencing directly will allow the prospect to admit a problem but take some of the sting out of admitting it directly to themselves. For example: *"A colleague and I are constantly going back and forth on the importance of this new technology. What do you think?"*

What will prevent you from using this technique is that you will want to go for the jugular and make your points decisively instead of subtly. Third party selling requires a little more tact, less ego, and more patience. It also requires the belief that your prospects frequently are smarter than you sometimes give them credit for.

When utilizing third party selling try to use examples that give your selling points balance and a sense of neutrality. By doing so, you gain credibility and trust. For example:

- *"Not everyone buys this argument, but some in the industry are saying this is the wave of the future. What do you think?"*
- *"Independent studies in the industry are showing conflicting results with this technology. What are your experiences?"*
- *"I know that some of our competitors are actively attacking this new technology. What is your company's stand on this technology?"*

Third party selling projects a non-selling posture of being fair and neutral. It also empowers the prospect to feel less pressure when they want to voice their opinions and allows the salesperson to get to the truth of the matter faster.

29

Never Badmouth Your Competition,
Let Your Prospects Do It for You

Managing your prospect's expectations and beliefs about your own offering is important. However, managing your prospect's expectations and beliefs about your competition can be even more critical, especially if you are involved in a hotly contested and competitive showdown. The trick is to do it subtly and professionally without losing credibility.

When we openly disparage our competition, we invalidate and dishonor our prospects and we project our own insecurities and doubts about the value we bring to the selling table. So instead of directly going after your competition, consider insinuating small morsels of doubt to get your prospect to formulate their own conclusions. Keep in mind that the best salesperson at the selling event is always the prospect. Let them sell themselves and reach the same conclusions that you'd like them to by prompting them with strategically crafted questions.

The following is a hypothetical scenario:

Your prospect met with your competition last week and they are sitting down with you for the first time. You have some clear advantages you want to highlight, and your competition has some real liabilities that you want to exploit. Here are some questions I use in my business to set up my competition that I know in advance will yield unsatisfying responses by my prospects. They also are effective in setting traps or landmines for my competition to stumble upon in the future:

- *"When you asked them about their specific plans for reinforcement of the training, what did they tell you?"*
- *"I'm curious... how much time did they spend learning about your problems as opposed to you learning about their training?"*
- *"When they told you that they were going to first assess and evaluate your team before they do the training, did you think that was a good idea?"*
- *"What kind of examples did they give you about their specialization of working exclusively with technology companies?"*

Invariably when I ask these questions the responses are frequently, *"They didn't bring that up"* and *"They couldn't sufficiently answer that."* To add insult to injury, I subtly respond, *"Is that a problem?";* *"Does that concern you?";* or *"Is that something you'd like to have?"* And then I follow up with asking them, *"Why do you want that?"* By avoiding a direct attack, I maintain my credibility and honor my prospect's past decisions.

Here are some generic questions and statements some of my clients have used in my classes to get the prospects emotionally involved and dig a deeper hole for themselves:

- *"I'm surprised you are dissatisfied with them. They generally have a good reputation."* Disagreeing with them will sometimes have them argue even more fervently on your behalf.
- *"What?"* This gets them to restate and repeat their frustration again.
- *"It doesn't sound bad enough to justify changing."*
- *"But you've been doing business with them for 10 years."*
- *"I assume when the problem came up that they immediately approached you, as opposed to you having to bring it to their attention?"*

By planting seeds of doubt and craftily laying landmines, you will never need to jeopardize or compromise your credibility by badmouthing your competition. In allowing your prospect to re-experience their frustration and verbalize their dissatisfaction, you will cause much more harm to your competition's position than if you were to directly challenge it yourself. Litigation lawyers know this tenet intimately. They are limited by procedure to only asking questions and not badgering the witness. So they build their case on the idea that the witness will trip up and sell themselves short. Just as in our legal system, the power of implication is so much more powerful than a direct assault.

30

Sales Letter: Recap the Prospect's Problems, Not How You Can Help Them

Here is an example of a follow-up letter that underscores the principles of change agent selling. Because prospects have an inherent need to be heard and understood, it is imperative to reflect back to your prospects your interpretations of their situation and their key issues. This reinforces the tenet that the salesperson who has the best understanding of a prospect's problem will consistently outsell the salesperson with the best solution. Notice there are no statements about us or our superior offering. They simply don't care. Our recap is all about their problems and their ensuing consequences. That's what they buy.

> October 28, 2004
> Kevin Davis
> Principal Corporation
> 5425 Miami Rd.
> Cincinnati, OH 45243
>
> Dear Kevin:
>
> Thank you for the time in allowing me to meet with you and Paul Jones. I appreciate your openness in discussing the future vision of Principal Corporation and I look forward to working with you in defining your sales process and helping you to grow your business.

Situation

Principal Corporation has been a very successful business. You have maintained an unprecedented impressive record of doubling sales every three years. You are looking to transition your business from a successful entrepreneurial driven business to a more process driven, professionally managed business. In looking to grow your business for the future, you have identified the need for more structure in your sales process, more sales management accountability, and a better handle on the strengths and weaknesses and future potential of your salespeople.

Key Issues

- o **Adapting to new markets** – You are entering new markets beyond your traditional markets and your team is going to face more competitive issues and challenging sales situations. Their skill sets will have to be upgraded in order to effectively compete.
- o **Target Accounts** – You are looking to segment more effectively key target accounts to go after. In order to accomplish this you will have to manage your salespeople closer and hold them more accountable.
- o **Lack of Process** – You want to institutionalize a more repeatable sales process and selling proposition that will allow you to better qualify selling opportunities in your pipeline and that will provide you with a more professional approach.
- o **CEO Mentality** – You would like your salespeople to act more like owners. As owners, they will have to have a much better selling strategy so that they can protect their assets of time, information, resources, relationships and self-esteem.
- o **Qualifying Opportunities** – Your sales team is too quick to demonstrate and propose and bid without first

qualifying the opportunities (find pain) and selling more strategically as opposed to transactionally.

○ **True Assessment of Sales Force** – Being new in your position, you want a better handle on the strengths and weaknesses of your sales team so you can grow it accordingly. Who has growth potential, who is open to change, who is willing to take risks, and who are your future players? Also it would be important to evaluate yourself to determine how to best optimize and maximize your sales management potential. Bottom line, after the assessment you will know who the right people are.

(The final step of the process is where you can apply your own process, proposal and investment.)

Our Process to Address Your Issues

(This is where you outline your process to address their problems.)

We propose the following:

(Outline and detail the specific steps to your proposal.)

Investment

(Detail the investment for your product or service.)

Kevin, I look forward to earning your trust and confidence and meeting with you and your general manager to review all the details.

Sincerely,

Rick Farrell

President

31

Guard Your Company Resources
as if They Were Your Own

Your resources are anything that cost your company money that you allocate to prospects. Most salespeoples' behavior reflects the belief that their company has infinite resources. One resource that is constantly abused by salespeople is manpower. Ask yourself how often do you use flimsy quotes and proposals that are prepared by estimating or by the technical department without any considerations for the cost? If you were the owner of your own company and you had to pay all those direct costs out of your pocket, you would probably think long and hard about doing it.

Your resources are your leverage. Allocate them according to when you can optimize your position. Look at your resources as an investment. Would I invest in this account if I knew I was vulnerable to a low probability of return? One of my machine tool distributors built a $500,000 state of the art demo room to demonstrate their equipment. The first month they were ecstatic with the activity it generated. Unfortunately, they soon realized that the salespeople booked the room with tire kickers and their two top producing salespeople could not schedule their two best accounts in for that month. Granted, they sold them the next month, but it did increase their cost of sales because their salespeople were not wisely utilizing their leverage.

Salespeople should guard their resources not because they are good corporate citizens who are concerned with costing the company money; they should guard their resources because it is their control and leverage point in the sale. Salespeople should adopt an owner mentality because if they allocate their resources wisely and accordingly, it will personally make them more productive and efficient. Ironically, what is good for the goose is good for the gander.

One resource that is very subtle but widely misused is references. References in theory cost you nothing in money and little in time. But they cost you tremendously in control if you allocate them at the wrong time. Use your references as a closing tool. Agree to give out references only at the optimal time when it will be the last thing prospects have to decide on and check on before they make their final decision. For example: *"Bill, I'd be happy to provide you with references. Since my customer's time is valuable, I have promised them that I won't misuse their time with prospects who aren't serious or who are still in the initial stages of checking us out. I have assured them that I won't use it as a prospecting tool but only as a closing tool. Does that sound fair to you?"* The beauty of this strategy is when I get resistance, I know I have a poorly qualified prospect.

One should have a desirability matrix to use on all prospects who are tapping your company's resources. Do they qualify for our resources and what is the likelihood of a positive return on the investment?

32

Guerrilla Marketing at Trade Shows:
Not for the Faint of Heart

If you think cold calling is nerve-racking and difficult, try working a trade show where you go booth to booth prospecting for business. I have seen highly competent salespeople in my business shudder at the idea of placing themselves in harm's way doing cold prospecting at a convention hall.

What make the task so daunting and intimidating are the signs and warnings waiting for you as you enter the hall: *"No soliciting exhibitors. Violators will be expelled."* Although I have never been expelled, I have had my share of harsh rebuffs from exhibitors.

What makes trade show selling (guerrilla marketing) worth the effort is the target-rich environment. Nowhere will you find 500+ companies under one roof, with many top decision makers in attendance and available, where you can glean very valuable information and intelligence.

Because the unofficial line at trade shows is that uninvited salespeople can be seen but not heard, you need to be very subtle, brief and to the point, respectful and humble. Unlike the code of waitresses, where at another restaurant they leave good tips and cheers to their fellow clan, salespeople tend not to extend the professional courtesy to uninvited salespeople in their booths. For many it is payback time. Believe me, I know. I have experienced hundreds of times where I was met by a salesperson manning the booth with anger and dismissal... like, *"How dare you walk into our hallowed space?"* Rightfully so, since they see you as an inconvenience and an intrusion. They can be a humorless bunch.

The Initial Approach

So as not to set you up for failure and humiliation, the following are some ideas, verbiage and some tactics to take the sting out of potentially putting yourself in harm's way. The strategy is to be non-intrusive, humble and unpredictably non-traditional.

- Prospect: *"How are you?"*
- Salesperson: *"Exhausted. This show is tough on the knees, but it can't be as tough as standing in place all day like you."*
- Salesperson: *"Do you mind if I ask you a stupid question? Worse yet, I'm not a prospect for you."*
- Prospect: *"There are no stupid questions."*
- Salesperson: *"Who is the VP of sales that I can send some information to?* (always infer that you are going to send information. They will feel less threatened when they decide to give you a name.) *I'm with Tangent. We are a sales training and development firm."*
- Salesperson: *"I don't suppose you'd be kind enough to point them out to me. Well thanks. I promise you I won't tell them you gave me their name."*

Generally if I go into 10 booths, I'll be able to speak to 3 decision makers. The percentages are similar to telephone cold calling, but they are a little better and of course here you get the benefit of meeting them face-to-face. My first six years in sales training, I went to an average of 40 trade shows a year in Chicago and secured all my business exclusively through trade show selling and marketing. It does work.

Qualify Decision Maker

Once I get in front of the decision maker, my goal is to be brief and be gone; and of course to qualify and disqualify them. I also want to build trust and differentiation with them through the quality of my professional approach.

The following is a simple example of my approach. The approach is very similar to a telephone cold call.

> *"One of your salespeople, whom I promised complete anonymity, pointed you out to me. I know you are very busy with the show here. I'm not sure if we could ever be of help to you. Can I very briefly tell you why I stopped by your booth, and you can tell me if we should go any further after that? We work with companies in helping them improve the effectiveness of their salespeople. Generally if someone like yourself would have a reason to talk with us after the show, it will be because you have issues in the following areas:*

> - *"Your salespeople are doing a good job with existing customers, but aren't bringing in new customers to grow the business to the next level.*
> - *"They are closing deals, but are leaving too much money on the table, causing the erosion of your margins.*
> - *"Your people are wasting a lot of valuable time doing wasteful quoting and proposing, resulting in higher cost of sales and longer selling cycles.*

> *"Are any of these issues coming up enough to justify us having a conversation now or in the future?"*

The whole idea is to secure a future follow-up call (face to face or telephone), or if things aren't too hectic in the booth and they seem to be open, to have a more in-depth conversation right there and then. Usually this will happen anywhere from 10% to 20%.

If I get shut down at this point and I have one last shot at them, I'll try the following last ditch questions before I do a full retreat:

- *"Has your company made a decision not to look at any new suppliers in this area?"*
- *"If there was a better way out there, and I'm not sure if we even have it, I'm guessing from your response you wouldn't be interested?"*
- *"Let me ask you a loaded and unfair question, if I may. Do you believe that what you've got is as good as it gets and it doesn't get any better? I told you it was unfair."*

Rarely do these questions get you any further than a confirmation that you are barking up the wrong tree. Anywhere from 5% to 10% of the time you will be able to get a positive outcome with these questions. The silver lining is, you know for sure the rest aren't a good prospect.

Alternative Approaches

Going booth to booth at trade shows can be intimidating for the uninitiated. Anything you can do to lighten your load and have fun at it will make it so much less stressful and more productive.

The following examples are ways to break the ice and to lighten things up a bit. It can get boring going to 60 booths in seven hours at a show, so you want to change things up just to keep your sanity and to stay fresh. All these examples are for a hostile person whom you are trying to defuse. The reality is, you'll run into some real jerks. So at least try to be playful, self-deprecating and unpredictable.

- *"I'm probably the last guy you wanted stopping by your booth today."*
- *"Please go easy on me, I'm terrible at this prospecting business."*
- *"Please don't gang up on me and take pot shots at the hapless, uninvited salesperson."*
- *"I'm afraid I'm not a prospect for your company. I'm afraid it is even worse – I'm a salesperson. If you allow me, I'll be brief and be gone."*

- *"The minute I walked in here I knew I was in trouble. Could you give me a brief reprieve here and then I'll be out of your hair? At least I can tell my boss I tried."*
- *"You are probably wondering why I'm still here."*
- *"You can probably guess this is a cold solicitation. Have you ever had to do them at a trade show? It isn't my preferred way of introduction. They aren't easy. Before you tell me your company wouldn't have any interest, can I ask you how many salespeople your company has?"*
- *"I'm visiting a couple of my customers here and I thought I'd stop by your booth to introduce myself. I hope I'm not intruding."*
- *"You are probably hit on by a lot by salespeople stopping by your booth trying to sell you their wares."*
- *"I'm guessing your company doesn't look very kindly on salespeople stopping by your booth to introduce themselves?"*
- *"By giving me their name, are you going to be violating a sacred company trust?"*
- *"I sense out of the goodness of your heart, you are protecting me because you are concerned that if I follow up with your company I'll get rejected."*
- *"Are you the official or unofficial company spokesperson on this issue?"*

Tough Qualifying Questions

The following is some verbiage to use on leads from a trade show, from Internet leads and for leads in general. There are subtle differences between lead follow-ups and cold calls. I find it useful to treat all leads as if they were a cold lead so that I don't assume anything, and so I do my due diligence regarding asking tough qualifying questions.

- *"So I can get a better idea of your business, would it be okay to ask you some specific questions about your company:*

  How many salespeople do you have?

  Are they all in Chicago?

171

Have you done training before?

What is the level of experience of your people?

Do you sell direct?

How are your people compensated?"

- *"Was there a specific reason you stopped by our booth, or did you just want some general information?"*
- *"Did you have an immediate need you wanted to discuss, or did you just want basic information for future needs?"*
- *"I'm following up on an inquiry that you made yesterday. What were you hoping we could help you with, or did you have any specific questions?"*
- *"I'm following up on an inquiry that you made yesterday on the Internet. We always take a realistic approach that until we know exactly what you want, we aren't specifically sure if we can help you or whether what we have is right for you. If it is alright with you, I'd like to ask you some questions to learn more about your company and why you initially called, and we can decide if we should go any further than that. First of all, how did you hear about us?"*
- *"Before I go into specifics, let me briefly outline where we've been a good fit for other companies and where we haven't been a good fit. We tend to be a good fit with companies who are experiencing issues with:*

> *Low margins due to salespeople not being able to maintain price integrity.*

> *Long selling cycles and higher costs of sales due to wasteful quoting and proposing.*

Stunted growth due to poor prospecting skills."

- *"We tend not to be a good fit for companies that aren't...* (enumerate all the reasons). *Which category closest fits your company's scenario?"*

The key to lead follow-up is to have a very defined sales process so that you aren't giving out a lot of information before you really get a feel for the prospect. This can be a little challenging because, since the prospect made the initial contact, they'll want to remain in control and get their needs met for getting information. They may not be accustomed to having a salesperson stepping back for moment and asking a lot of questions before they give information. The guideline I use to have balance is to look at it as an exchange or a give and take. If they aren't willing to share any information, then that should be a real red flag.

33

Phrases and Questions that Will
Kill Trust and Lose Sales

The Kiss of Death:

In the information economy, the language and phrases you use will either advance your cause or cost you support, trust and sales. The following are my favorite annoying stereotypical phrases, statements and questions that will identify you as an amateur, narcissist, self-serving and company-centric salesperson. Some of the following are merely trite and others are very counterproductive in building trusting relationships.

> *"We want to help you find a solution to fit your 'needs'."* -- So cliché

> *"How are you?"* -- Unsolicited chitchat doesn't work as well today

> *"Is Tuesday at 8:00 good for you or is Friday at 3:00 better?"* -- Old school

> *"Would you like it in red or blue?"* -- More old school

> *"You do want to save money, don't you?"* -- Leading the witness, and insulting

> *"Are you the decision maker?"* -- Overbearing

"Is it okay with you that I keep in touch with you monthly to see if anything changes?" -- Needy

"I'd be happy to send out some literature on our exciting new product." -- Just as needy

"Let me be honest with you." -- The other times you weren't?

"If I can show you a way to solve your problems today, will you be in a position to buy?" --

Of course they'll say yes. It's too easy.

"We'd like to partner with you." -- Too cliché

"I wanted to see if we could be of help to you." -- Just as cliché

"Did I reach you at a good time?" -- You sound like everyone else. Too subservient.

"We can give you a better price. Can I send you a quote?" -- Commodity seller

"Thanks for taking time to meet with me." -- Too subservient

"I'm not trying to sell you anything." -- Yeah… right!

"I wanted to tell you about our new product." -- Who cares about you?

"My solution is the one that best fits your needs." -- Says who?

"I know how you feel. Many have felt the same way. Most have found…" -- Not bad, if everyone didn't say it.

These old school techniques were probably effective during their time. In today's business climate, customers so often don't extend salespeople the benefit of the doubt. An old school phrase or question here and there and you've lost rapport. This is why customers in general don't see salespeople as equals and worthy of their precious time. Some of these phrases aren't so bad, but they are so overused that you start to look and sound like everyone else. And that is the "kiss of death" in sales.

34

The Seven Deadly Sins Of Highly Ineffective Salespeople

The seven deadly sins of highly ineffective salespeople are: control, narcissism, over-selling, too much emotion, need for approval, lack of personal responsibility and undo excess (time, information, persistence). These sins only become problematic when they are taken to extremes. I purposely choose this list of transgressions because they are non-intuitive, contrary and controversial. They underline some of the most divisive beliefs that will make a salesperson's career a living hell. I could have shown the typical list of too much talking, not listening, no sales process, etc., but they are pedestrian and predictable.

The original seven deadly sins are: superbia, ira, invidia, avaritia, gula, acedia, and luxuria. Or, in order: pride, anger, envy, greed, gluttony, sloth, and lust. So here are Tangent Knowledge System's seven deadly sins of highly ineffective salespeople:

The Sin of Control

Savvy salespeople know that the way you gain control is… you give it up. When we are too controlling in the sales process, we end up being controlled by the control we seek. Seeking control becomes counter-productive and unrealistic.

The average salesperson tries too hard; the exceptional salesperson doesn't. Intelligent and selective effort attracts customers; over-the-board effort and control detracts. Salespeople who learn to adopt this posture become lazy like a fox.

We think we are in control of a sales call, but we really aren't. We think we know what is best for our customers, but we don't. We think we can accurately interpret their lack of responses, but we can't. The good news is that once we realize all this, the mystery of selling is greatly diminished.

We mistakenly confuse giving up control for weakness and seizing control for strength. Actually the inverse is true. I like to refer to giving up control as the non-selling posture: Nothing to prove, nothing to disprove. It is non-dogmatic and non-authoritative. It allows customers the authority, the control and the independence to seek their own answers and conclusions independent of the salesperson's selling agenda.

In sales, it is imperative that we give up control and temper our need for recognition, validation, to stand out and to truly be heard and listened to, so that we don't compete and overshadow our customer's exact same needs. Nothing strengthens your customer's sense of being in control and sense of self than being right. Strive to consistently make your customer right. Customers will have a strong need to make you wrong when they don't feel in control or feel they are right.

So the purpose of the non-selling posture is to get your customer to change their ego-state to a less demanding and inflexible posture. Customers are far more willing to be open, frank and share the truth with you if they believe they are in control. The non-selling posture works so well because it asks so little in return.

The non-selling posture takes the position that you don't know what is best for your customer. As long as you don't know what is best for them, you'll spend a lot of time, care, empathy and focus on trying to find out. The better you get at selling this way, the less you appear to be selling. Average salespeople use their ego to sell, and it gets them only average results.

The ultimate journey to giving up control is giving your customer permission and in some cases, encouragement to give you a "no." If you think giving up an addiction like crack is difficult, try giving up control and going for "no." *"No, the word you have been trained to fear, is, in fact, the word that will change your life for the better, forever,"* says Jim Lamp.

The problem with the way most salespeople sell is that the more enthusiastic, positive, best foot forward, excited, optimistic and, yes, subjective you are, the more vulnerable you will be to getting "yes'd to death." Traditional selling is unfortunately fear-based selling. It is eternal optimism run amok. A non-selling posture invites "no" as a viable and realistic outcome. The non-selling posture and giving up control is built on the foundation of good business decisions and not rampaging emotions, wild assumptions and unrealistic expectations. If you can't get a customer to commit to say "yes," see if you can get them to commit to say "no."

The Sin of Selling

Selling by its very nature produces so often the exact opposite effect. Selling is repelling. The harder you sell, the harder it is to sell. Selling has nothing to do with selling; selling has everything to do with asking thought-provoking questions and honoring your customer with incisive listening.

Feature and benefit selling represents the granddaddy of them all as the biggest offender of the sin of selling. Most companies and their salespeople covet their value-add, their features and benefits, and their value proposition as if it were the Holy Grail. The reality is that all value propositions are inherently valueless. The feature and benefit style of selling that has served companies so well in the past, no longer works. It is tried, but no longer true.

Value-added (feature and benefits) selling is rooted in old economic conditions using time-honored traditions; a sales strategy from another era entirely; some unimaginable distant epoch of 5-10 years ago. This artificial style of selling that, until recently, has withstood the test of time only homogenizes your offering. Value proposition selling is just roll-the-dice selling; you are on autopilot and you cross your fingers and show up and throw up. It is driven by the love to talk and the fear to listen. It is jargon on crack.

Salespeople operate under the quaint notion that it is their God-given right to sell their features and benefits. Since it states in the Sales Constitution that all products are not created equal, it is your solemn right and salesperson duty to show customers the correct way to the Promised Land. However, the reality is that no one has the corner on absolute truth.

The irony is that all companies, big or small, sophisticated or unworldly, in all industries, covering all products and all services, intangibles or tangibles, sell the same way. They sanitize and whitewash their offering by using common standards, open architecture specifications that multiple vendors can easily meet. In the end, it becomes a wash. The very thing that feature and benefit selling tries to protect against, it reinforces. Salespeople's self-indulgent presentations reflect mostly minimum standards and lowest common denominators for being considered or just staying in business. It is truly a zero-sum game.

In the knowledge-based economy, the value of a salesperson is judged not on what they know about their product, but on what they can learn about their customers' problems and critical success factors. Unlike the Dark Ages, leading with your product information and solutions is now looked upon with suspicion.

In the Internet era, sales organizations can no longer get away with placing pathetic faith and stock in their products and solutions. We eulogize and romanticize our products and service offerings as if they were the end all, the real thing. We can no longer afford to treat customers as Pavlovian dogs that are trained to respond to only one stimulus – our features and benefits. All products and services are intrinsically valueless. We need to put more faith and value into our customers' problems and their corresponding consequences, and learning the intricacies of their business.

The reason sales can appear to be so challenging and difficult is because we carry this heavy burden of proof around. The more we think we must sell our product's features and benefits, the less we sell. It is a cruel joke of the universe. Ironically, the reason we do not change is because we would feel so guilty at how easy it is by not selling – it would grate against our Puritan work ethic. We would feel so cheated and shortchanged by patiently sitting back, listening, observing, questioning, and letting the customer proactively do all the selling as to why or why not they would be open to changing. What would you do if you no longer had to be in charge? We take the path of most resistance because we feel in control, we hate to listen, we are self-absorbed and we love to convince and persuade, even when it is not necessary.

As soon as salespeople conclude that they have nothing inherently special or unique to sell, that is when they will truly differentiate themselves from the competition and not have to rely on a flawed style of selling, such as features and benefits selling. We should no longer treat our product as if it were the means to an end. Our product and its attributes are simply a vehicle to help us build trust and respect by learning about our customer's business.

The Sin of Excess

Persistence, time and overload of information represent the sins of excess. Any positive action taken to an extreme produces the exact opposite effect. That is the exact case with the sin of excess. The antidote for the sin of excess is, less is more.

Too many well-intended salespeople have been schooled in the notion that a good salesperson never quits. Actually, the difference between a professional and an amateur is that a professional gives up early, easily and effortlessly on losing causes. The problem is that too many salespeople use persistence as a tool to mask poor selling skills and strategies.

PERSISTENCE

Raw, indiscriminate persistence doesn't work like it used to work in the information economy because of the sheer technological barriers. How can you hope to be efficient and effective while at the same time be persistent with customers who hide behind email, national do not call lists, voicemail, caller ID and an electronic secretary that has you announce your name.

For persistence to be effective, it has to be targeted and focused. I know way too many salespeople who are extremely persistent with customers who have no money, no authority, no budget and no problems, but are more than happy to lead these gullible salespeople astray. Also, the harder you pursue, the more you try to control, the less your customer feels in control, the more they feel compelled to push you away.

Too many salespeople are guided by a private code or gospel of productivity, aimless busy work or avoidance activity. When you unshackle yourself from a superstitious reverence for the mysterious god named productivity (persistence), you can actually get a lot of focused work done. Customers generally have stronger resistance than salespeople have stamina.

TIME

The sin of excess also applies to wasteful allocation of time. We spend too much time with the wrong opportunities and not enough time with the right opportunities.

Ever-shortening product life cycles due to rapid technological advancements in the global economy are causing virtually every product and service to quickly become a commodity. Given the warp speed economy in which we do business, nothing is more important in salespeople's work life than time.

Time is your single most important leverage. Unfortunately, it is a depreciating asset that is non-recoverable. Once you've given it away, you can never get it back. Since time is money, you should be discriminating as to whom, when and under what circumstances you should allocate it. Not only do we have to manage spending time on the right people, we also have to work to shorten the length of time it takes to sell to people. Equally important is the time it takes to lose deals. Too often salespeople operate under the belief that *"my time isn't as valuable as yours."* They would rather patiently wait for the occasional bones or crumbs that customers throw their way than go out and look for better opportunities. Customers receive this unintended message and they have no problem having you go on unending fools' errands. Many salespeople would rather chase opportunities in the face of insurmountable odds and face inevitable failure than to prospect for new business. A lot of misdirected use of time is simply avoidance activity. There will always be more opportunities to invest in than there are time and resources. Therefore, salespeople should be discriminatory and selective with their time.

Time kills all deals, and shortening the selling cycle is critical to managing time. The longer deals sit out there, the greater the chance they will go south. Most salespeople operate under the exact opposite assumption. They operate under a false sense of security that if they persist, outlast the competition, show the customer they care, and are assertive, they will ultimately prevail. In reality, this is simply not true. Professional salespeople are good at qualifying their opportunities and cutting their losses when they are operating under non-optimal conditions. They know there are only two winners in a competitive selling situation: the salesperson who was awarded the deal and the salesperson who lost early and saved time.

In today's marketplace, selling is more about sifting, sorting and selecting opportunities that have the greatest likelihood of closing, as opposed to always trying to sell, convince, persuade and cajole. Salespeople who take on a business owner mentality look at acquisition costs as overhead that needs to be judiciously guarded and protected. Unfortunately, 80% of what salespeople are spending their time on has a low value. Working in this way is a waste of your most valuable asset of time, and is not consistent with a business owner's mentality.

Time should also be viewed as an inventory control system. A business owner who looks at inventory has one thing in mind: turn it as quickly as possible, because time is money. A salesperson with a business owner mentality sees their sales pipeline in the same way. They must move their customers quickly and profitably through their pipeline while at the same time keeping them comfortable and feeling no pressure. A poor inventory control system in sales is a surplus in the pipeline of accounts that aren't viable, closeable and moving in a timely fashion. Time-oriented salespeople know that the longer it takes to sell to customers, the less time and money they have to invest elsewhere.

MISALLOCATION AND OVERLOADING OF INFORMATION

The last sin of excess is misallocation of information. Salespeople give too much, too soon without any consideration as to its cost.

Information is your intellectual capital. Salespeople with a business owner mentality plays their cards close to the chest and judiciously guard and protect their information and dispense with it sparingly. As John Hirth says, *"What you know can hurt you."* The problem with all of our precious and hard-won information is that there is an over-tendency to want to give it out early, often and prematurely, resulting in salespeople being reduced to "free consultants." To minimize free consulting, guard your asset of information. You allocate your information when your customer is in a position to make decisions. Your information represents your leverage and control points in the sales cycle. In the past, salespeople's value was firmly established by the information they brought to the table. The information economy has changed all that. Since information is accessible freely and widely, salespeople's value proposition has been neutralized and marginalized. Salespeople's mandate now should be to get information, not give it. This totally changes the dynamics of a typical sales call.

You are now paid and rewarded for your questions, not your answers. No longer can you afford to build a product case; you have to build a business case that is heavily influenced by your ability to garner important, privileged and sensitive information from your customer.

Selling is more about what you don't know versus what you do know. The customer's information carries the most weight. Yet, salespeople act as if their information is king and they invariably overplay their hand, in turn diminishing the importance and dignity of their customer.

The Sin of Lack of Personal Responsibility

Salespeople who don't take personal responsibility for their results don't grow... period. The beauty of not taking personal responsibility is that you don't have to change, and you get the distinct pleasure of pointing the finger.

The more you justify your failures and point the finger, the more you hold on to them, the greater the likelihood you will simply recycle them. Taking ownership and responsibility always empowers us. Denying responsibility will always disempower us.

The ability to take responsibility also allows you to not take things so personally. When you take 100% responsibility for rejection in sales, it can be very liberating because all our negative thoughts that we entertain are always putting the blame elsewhere. Since our own self-worth only comes from the internal, blaming outside circumstances is simply giving up responsibility. Our merit is the cause of everything it feels and thinks. Our mind therefore is the only thing we can legitimately blame.

The Sin of Emotion

Salespeople who can't control their emotions lose perspective in a sales call. They lose objectivity and patience and can't properly determine if they have a qualified customer. Because they are so emotionally involved, they don't listen and they miss out on critical information.

Salespeople who are emotionally invested in a deal tend to be overly persistent, waste time, and crash and burn when they get negative information. Keep in mind, the salesperson that is the least emotionally invested in the outcome of a sale will consistently outsell the salesperson who is the most enthusiastic and gung-ho.

Salespeople who aren't emotionally invested in the sales interaction are neutral, unbiased and aren't afraid to hear "no" – they actually encourage it in some cases. They sell from a business strategist position and build a business case for change, not a product case. They have a quiet confidence instead of an overly emotional posture, so they minimize all the typical static of self-talk: *"I wonder when they'll make up their mind; what if I don't make this sale; what am I going to spend my commission check on; what am I going to do if they want to think it over?"*

The Sin of Narcissism

Narcissistic salespeople are self-centered, company and product-centered and lack self-awareness. They believe in the art of enthusiasm in a sales call. They aren't aware that this traditional sales strategy has a fatal flaw – you can't be enthusiastic and gung-ho and be customer-centric and understanding at the same time. How can you ask insightful questions that get to the core of your customer's business and problems and be enthusiastic and upbeat at the same time? It's totally out of context.

The Sin of Approval

The classic portrayal of a salesperson is someone who is very enthusiastic and friendly; wants people to like them; is persuasive and talkative; and is intelligent and persistent. The problem is, most salespeople have taken this art form to an extreme. They aren't willing to challenge customers and risk losing approval. They avoid asking tough questions that will get them the truth. They shy away from healthy confrontation and getting their own needs met as opposed to getting the more important need of making the sale. They are more concerned that customers like them rather than respect them. These types are constantly used by their customers for their expertise and solutions.

CONCLUSION

The sevens sins of highly ineffective salespeople represent mindsets and strategies that are flawed and put salespeople at a severe disadvantage. These transgressions put too much focus on the wrong party: the salesperson and their product. In order to be more productive and effective salespeople need to be able to maximize their time and manage their information more effectively. And they need to give up the hope of controlling the sales process and being too emotionally vested in the outcome of the sale.

35

To Change or Not to Change is the Question for Customers

The change-agent strategy is a process of creative destruction and self-selection on the part of the customer and the sales person. It is a process of qualifying business fit and relationship chemistry.

Selling is more about undoing than doing. It is not about selling, or even solving a problem, as much as it is about unraveling the mystery behind the customer's circumstances, unique vantage point and priorities. All customers experience gap management issues; I am here, andI really want to be there.

Change-agents professionally meddle in their customer's business to see if change can be justified. Classic feature and benefit sellers meddle in the customer's business to change their minds. Change-agents start with a hypothesis. Information sellers start with irrefutable statements of fact backed up by their proof of concept. Good luck with that!

Anyone today can go to the Internet and Google their problem and 8000 results will flash before their eyes. But the Internet has done nothing to help customers first define and assess the consequences of their problems, to understand the cost of changing and to make sense of the overwhelming amount of information that they have access to.

The change-agent is not concerned with the "what" (solution), but the "why" and the "how." It is not what they want, but why they want it, and how they will be affected by change that are the real issues change-agents care about. And by the way what customers really care about most is avoiding problems more than capitalizing on opportunities.

According to The HR Chally Group customers rate (39%) the sales person's effectiveness as their number one criteria for selecting a product or service. The value of the change-agent is there context, not their content.

Change-agents look at the big picture of their customer's business, not just their immediate needs. They run the call like a business meeting, not like a sales meeting. Background information is critical to them. They take the time to find out what it is like to be their customer, what they are personally wrestling with, what are their conflicted interests and what they are really concerned with. It takes a lot of focus, business chops, energy and non-biased analysis to take their customer through this process.

Through their soft sell strategy, the change-agent tries to mediate the burdensome conflicts of interest that hover over all sales calls; the customer wants to give as little information as possible and spend as little time as possible, while the traditional, stereotypical sales person wants to give out as much information as possible, spin it and take up as much of the customer's time as possible. Both these agendas represent the foundation for mistrust and inefficiency.

Change-agents are into delayed gratification and so are their customers, assuming there is trust. So long as they are helping their customers look at their challenges differently, spending their time wisely, solution and product information is premature and specious. Because customers so often do not really know what they want, why they want it, and what they are trying to avoid until the very latter part of the sales call, anything you give them beforehand is suspect and possibly confusing.

36

Enthusiasm Creates Value for the Seller and Little for the Customer

You want to try to personally and emotionally connect with your customer on an individual level, while at the same time depersonalizing your offering so customers will not force feed you answers that they know you want to hear.

Without evolved sensitivity to another's opinion, empathy, sincerity and basic humility, the non-selling posture will fall on its face and be disastrous. Empathy is the most underrated, undervalued and underutilized skill set for sales people in the information economy. Enthusiasm, excitement, eagerness, being Mr Feel-Good and overflowing optimism are the most over utilized and least productive skill sets, because it is about delivering content and not what is really most important to customers; context and perspective.

In the healthcare field they now train doctors in empathy because not only does it lower litigation, but it increases the efficacy of the care to patients. The same is true in the world of selling. We are paid and rewarded more to feel than we are to think in sales and to get our customers to feel more than to just logically think.

Once your ego is engaged and on high alert, all bets are off in a sales call. Sales people's egotistical position only heightens the defenses of their customer's egotistical position. We all know how challenging and frustrating it can be to have a constructive conversation with a customer whose ego is fully engaged. The primary purpose of the non-selling posture is to help sales people minimize ego, self-interest, self-reference and be expectation free and hyperrealistic.

Being a hyperrealist is subversive to many conventional sales people because most sell in an unrealistic, ideal and romantic world where customers pretend to pay attention, find sales people's pitches memorable and inspiring, freely share the truth, do not prevaricate or manipulate and love to have sales people influence their choices.

The non-selling posture is a reaction to the fact that in the information economy customers share little information to sales people, do not inform them that they are pursuing a lost cause, rarely give them the privilege of saying they are not interested, or giving the sales person the peace of mind of closure. Customers rightfully justify their actions in many cases because they get so little value and professional respect out of the sales interaction, and they know that sales people are primarily operating from their own self-interest. So they have no qualms about returning the favor.

"A man's sense of self is defined through his ability to achieve results," says John Gray. Sales people have a fierce competitive spirit and love to win. Unfortunately, they are perceived by customers of wanting to win at their expense. However, customers and sales people both win regardless of the outcome when goals are defined, problems are isolated, costs are assessed, the cost of change is fully discussed and the priority of changing is fully explored. Selling is not persuasion, it is about helping customers decide what is in their best interests. That is the essence of the non-selling posture.

Because of their strong self-interest in defining themselves in making the sale, sales people are viewed as non-credible and apathetic. Most sales people have to be shown how to be trustworthy, credible, insightful and empathetic. The non-selling posture is an artificial insemination of empathy that forces the sales person to listen with care, restrain their pitch, create value by having customers look at their business differently, and allow the customer to find their own answers independent of the sales person's self-interest.

Sales people need to reengineer the way they think about selling, building trust, assessing opportunities and their role as a facilitator. Once they think differently and their intent to help the customer is authentic, the words will come naturally. If sales people sold where they were not emotionally involved in the outcome, they would begin to really create value as trusted advisors.

37

Be Wary of Commitment Phobics

The great recession of 2008 has created a highly evolved master of BS and spin. As customers take longer to make decisions, take fewer risks and want to leave their options open, they must keep sales people under the ether of false hope and absolute delusion to keep them engaged.

Oh my...where did they learn such subtle language of deception? Prospects have truly mastered the art of mumbo-jumbo and double talk. I'm absolutely convinced they don't even know that they're consciously doing it because their toneality and their posture doesn't change much in their delivery. In other words there is no obvious tell. Yet it's there. They can deliver the biggest line of nonsense without even flinching.

Don't get me wrong, these aren't bad people. It's just a function of the times. The bottom line is they're information hijackers and rustlers. Their daily existence relies on extracting information from unsuspecting sales people. These types of customers justify their existence with your information. You'll generally find these folks at lower levels, who else has the time to do it otherwise.

If you're not careful the information highwaymen will woefully waste your time, energy and resources, and most importantly your tenuous sense of hope and promise. They'll browbeat you at a drop of a hat to be able to put you into their hip pocket for possible future use. They're so frustrating to deal with because they blow hot and cold at the same level to keep you guessing. As long as you're in constant limbo they can gain the greatest leverage from you.

The following are some typical passive aggressive responses and statements that you'll find. By themselves they're not so bad. But, the true virtuosos are able to deliver them in succession without missing a beat. These types of prospects refuse to be pinned down, or take any position that is positive or negative. They're commitment phobic and thrive on keeping open all their options. Their true talent lies in their ability to give these forthcoming statements with the coldness of an undertaker. Their posture of neutrality gives sales people virtually nothing to sink their teeth into:

- We would never want to rule out the possibility.
- It's a definite maybe.
- There's a strong likelihood down the road, in the near future, if everything remains the same and nothing changes, we'll be interested.
- The answer is not a no, but not a yes.
- It's kind of hard to tell. It sort of depends.
- We never like to close the door on new ideas.
- It varies. You never know what will happen.
- Send us some information and let's see what happens and we'll go from there.
- You're more than welcome to send some information. We'll keep it in our files.

You have nothing to lose by participating in the bid.

- We never like to say never.
- I can't believe you'll lose, but I can't guarantee you'll win.

I'd hate to tell you no. You just never know.

In order to neutralize this very deceptive strategy, sales people have to go heavily into their "buyer's mode." They have to screen, heavily qualify and disqualify customer statements and positions just like a customer/ prospect would do with a sales person. You have to have a talent to collaborate, authenticate and substantiate. You have to understand that you can't take anything at face value. Half of selling is learning what to buy or not to buy regarding customer's statements; fact or crap.

The following are beliefs, metaphors, loose rules and strategies that will help sales people minimize and prevent prospects from leading them down the primrose path of false hope and having them needlessly jumping through hoops:

- There are always two winners at every selling event; the deal winner, and the other who lost quickly, easily and with minimal expenditure of resources.
- You must be willing to lose. The more spin and BS they give you the more you must be willing to press for a resolution; pro or con. For example; I'm hearing you have a genuine sincere interest to change, but because of poor timing and circumstances beyond your control, you have just a casual interest now to take action. How accurate is that for your situation?"
- You must have a strong pipeline of deals and a healthy backlog of prospects to be able to stand your ground and not be pushed around, otherwise it is just false posturing.
- You can't live in a cloistered world of Nirvana where false hopes and flimsy promises flourish.
- Keep records and be a diligent chronicler. Keep track of all the deals that you pursue that are flimsy and long-shots and see what your hit rate is. If you're honest with yourself you'll probably realize that you were a stereotypical sales person who was operating under the false tenet that hope springs eternal in the peddler's heart.
- Be a realist.
- Always be closing for the truth. Be in love with the truth; not with your offering.
- Your job isn't to sell. Your job is to get customers to make tough decisions.
- Be balanced in your sales approach. Bring up pros and cons.
- Be a master of reading between the lines. Listen strongly for what isn't being said.

- Be wary of unemotional language. It's frequently a tell for lack of commitment.
- If customers are unwilling to be fully engaged and share useful, sensitive and important information you must question their level of intent. If they don't value your context, input, advice and perspective, you have very little to sell.
- Don't sell with a scarcity mentality. Neediness is a foul smelling cologne.
- Let the answer and possibility of "no" be at the forefront of your sales strategy. You can't define and confirm a "yes" response without making "no" an available and accessible answer.
- The harder you sell, the harder it is to sell and get to the truth. Selling by its very nature so often produces the exact opposite effect.
- Learn to throw out early every realistic hurdle and potential deal killer. Match them tit for tat. The more delusional prospects are with their spin, the more you're willing to keep them honest by really challenging them professionally.
- Selling at a higher level in many cases is more about buying than selling. Be as discriminating and discerning of the information that your customers provide you, as they are of the information you provide them.
- Validate! Validate! Validate!
- Be a master qualifier and then learn to be a black belt disqualifier. Selling is more about sifting, sorting and selecting as opposed to selling and convincing in the information economy.
- Have the posture that you're always "willing to walk." It will do wonders for your confidence.
- Don't be an "eager beaver." Sales people with unbridled excitement, enthusiasm and optimism lose objectivity and are highly susceptible to spin and false hope.

Once you realize that selling isn't so much about convincing and persuading, but more about identifying prospects that are ready to buy, selling becomes a lot more rewarding and fulfilling. Sales people have to pick their battles effectively. Winning isn't just about being awarded the deal, it's also about winning efficiently.

Prospects will continue to prey upon sales people who have the strategy of "hope springs eternal in the peddlers heart," until they are able to deal with customers who stonewall and filibuster them to death. Sales people have to understand the difference between a yes and getting yes to death.

38

Customers Hate and Love Change at the Same Time

It is very common for customers to experience cognitive dissonance when they are considering change. Cognitive dissonance is an uncomfortable feeling caused by holding contradictory ideas simultaneously. Customers face a quandary when it comes to change.

The change-agent helps facilitate the internal discussion customers have with themselves and the outside discussion they will inevitably have with the other stakeholders and decision influencers in their company. They help customers vocalize the negatives and the positives of change. When you help customers come to terms with their hesitations, doubts and fears you tend to get to the truth quicker, build trust and disqualify customers who have the twin evil forces of change; they have the will, but not the means, they have the means, but not the will.

A change-centric sales person realizes that their biggest competition and challenge is first and foremost share of mind and the status quo. To help your customer assess the options of change, you must first help them disprove their current method and process. The customer needs to be the lead on this exercise. Unfortunately, sales people love to lead customers to their own self-serving, foregone conclusions. They want to build a solution without first tearing apart and dismantling the existing structure. You need to deconstruct before you can construct.

You are the sale. If the customer will not allow you to consult, then you offer little value other than your deliverables. If your advice is not needed then you enter the realm of a commodity player. In the information economy, a commodity, sales person's job is in large part being replaced by a more cost effective seller...the Internet.

To be an effective change-agent you need to enter early in the customer's process. The problem must be challenging or time consuming enough to warrant outside influence and insight. If the customer has the confidence to independently do their own digging, identifying, problem analysis, change analysis and is supremely confident in their own council, you have very little to bring to the table other than product placement. Customers must be open to an integrated offering of professional expertise and product delivery and must be willing to pay for it in time and in cost. This hybrid approach still represents a very viable sales strategy even in the information economy with customers who aren't procurement oriented.

Change can't be conducted by a bowl in a china shop mentality. Change is like a fragile game of stick. It must be built slowly, one stick at a time and in an orderly manner. Look at selling as pull marketing, instead of push selling. When you fully pull out all the whys (motive for change), the what (solution) becomes a lot easier to reconcile and explain.

Mainstream sellers focus their efforts on the least important part of the sale – proof of concept. They're working on the wrong end of the equation. Their primary focus should be on threat identification, problem appraisal, cost of implementation, timing, cost of dismantling existing solutions, the emotional and psychological cost of the inconvenience and disruption of change and integrating the new with the old.

Change-agents are keen to point out to their customers that time, money and resources spent on one initiative can't be spent on another. They collaborate with customers to do damage control, scrutinize customer's motives for change and look at all associated risks. They aren't afraid to play Chris Kringle on Miracle on 34th St. where they point out various options, choices and directions.

Your desire and ability to help your customer really understand their business will come from a position of acceptance rather than an application of will. Too many sales people apply coercion in their positive intent to help and they often achieve the exact opposite effect. To really help someone, and play the role of a change-agent, you must give up your cherished opinions, expectations, sense of pride and divorce and distance yourself from outcomes that are predominantly in your own self-interest. Most sales people's pride impedes their ability to be a neutral change-agent.

39

Feature and Benefit Sellers: Victims of Their Own Success

Information product pushing can be nicely summed up by the idea that customers are not buying what you are selling like they used to. Not because you do not know your product, or how to communicate it well. It is because you do not know their business issues. It is because you do not give them the platform to intelligently communicate them.

Mainline sales people have to learn to realize that their phantom and iron grip on their information is not working. They need to refocus their attention to their customer's information platform including challenges, problems, and negative consequences of those problems.

Feature and benefit selling is fully complicit with information overload and compounds all its problems. The very best thing you can say about feature and benefit selling is it does not make your position worse, it just does not make it better. And if it does not make it better, it really defeats the whole purpose – does it not?

Feature and benefit selling is the height of recirculating and repackaging of used, mundane and spurious ideas. To make matters worse, product pushers are very indiscreet as to with whom, when, where and under what conditions they should spread the good word. Feature and benefit sellers simply are a walking argument for restraint because it is the quickest way to be reduced to column fodder, the reverse of its purported mandate.

Feature and benefit sellers are a victim of their own success. In their well intended rush to educate they get caught in the crossfire of too much information. It is a classic, double edge sword.

A lot of feature and benefit sellers attempt to trade up to consultative selling to escape the commodity trap, but so often it ends up to be a poor substitute because all they really are doing is denying their undying need to sell, convince and persuade. It is a hard habit to break. You really have to be willing to totally change your reference from me to you.

I was at a commencement event for my nephew at an art school where the speaker said love the art in yourself, instead of loving yourself and your art. Always being the consummate sales trainer, I thought how does this fit in the world of sales.

This is what I determined. Love the pursuit of knowledge and the understanding of your customer, but do not have your customer see you are in love with your product and company at their detriment. When you are in love with your product, you are at risk of becoming tone deaf to the customer's information and priorities.

Product selling dulls senses, dulls your empathy, dulls your imagination, makes you a dullard, and it dwarfs your customer. It also has you living vicariously through your product, instead of being a customer activist. When you are not a customer activist you spend too much effort trying to get a customer and too often you end up acquiring a new competitor and having to find a new prospect.

Selling is storytelling at its finest hour. Tell customers you want to swap stories. Let them go first to determine if your story will have any relevance. The less inclined they are to go first, the greater you start off at a deficit. The best story will always be the customers. Next in line is the story of how your product/service addresses their major problems. So simply reconstitute your features and benefits to a storyline that is all about the customer's problems with little need to touch upon your solution until problems are firmly established and assessed.

40

Problems Shape Solutions

Prospects do not see reality, rather they pre-perceive it. Usually all they see is memory, the past, their beliefs and expectations. That is why it is so important when you are doing problem shooting to go very deep into their past problems.

Typically corporate resolution of problems are ultimately done for pure selfish reasons by your customer. To see the truth, to see reality, and to see things accurately from your customer's personal perspective you have to figure out their emotional investment in change, and their own personal stake. Stop selling to a faceless, corporate entity. Who you really are selling to are individuals and people who happen to work for corporations.

All problems are significant or insignificant relative to other problems. Find out what their other problems are, especially if it does not relate specifically to your application. Once you find out what is broken you need to break it again to give your customer's personal perspective. In other words, you need to reverse tracks to revisit the problem, and break it down so the customer can reevaluate and reexperience it for the significance of its cost, impact, negative consequences and actionability.

Remember, every sale has basic obstacles; no problem, no means, no authority, no urgency, poor timing and fierce competing initiatives vying for limited resources.

Be a doubting Thomas. Act as if you were from Missouri (show me state). Do not take anything at face value. This is where you really bring value to the table. Question customer's problems as to whether they are really actionable. Cover all your bases and theirs. Make sure you know what they have to gain or lose.

The daily struggle is an elixir that puts them in their comfort zone. They are comfortably uncomfortable, and often no amount of facts and figures, or gentle arm twisting will get them to see the light.

Conventional sales people are avid followers of the cult of positive thinking; always be positive, energized, excited, optimistic and always look at things from the bright side. This is a great way to live your life, do not get me wrong. There is definitely a time and place for it in sales, especially when you have to deal with all the ups and downs.

However, when energized and optimistic selling runs constantly through your veins, it is very hard to transition from always looking at things from a positive angle, to now looking and dwelling on customer's problems, fears, insecurities and doubts.

The irony is for a customer to have a positive buying experience you have to help them look at the negatives of their situation. If you are going to be a trusted and credible advisor you are going to have to find a delicate balance of the two.

41

Selling With Extreme Prejudice
and Without Probable Cause

I love and hate clichés as much as the next person. The following short list of clichés are some of the biggest challenges and risks sales people face in today's selling environment of mistrust and outdated selling strategies:

- Customers have a lot more say in whether they buy or not, than we as sales people have a say in whether we sell or not. Having the right solution is not nearly as important as being with the right customer, with the right problem, with the right timing, with the right authority, and the right means.
- Customers do not care how much you know until they know how much you care. If you believed this, you would think long and hard before you lifted your finger a centimeter off the table as to whether it was worth the energy and time to launch into your proactive selling campaign. No more preemptive selling barrages.
- Seek first to understand before being understood. Selling is an understanding business, not a being understood business. No one cares about us, our product, or our company. They only rightfully care about themselves. The only person that cares about us is our mother. Stop being self-centered and product-centered in your sales approach.
- You cannot sell anything to anyone. You can only provide a conducive environment for them to self-motivate themselves. Stop pushing product and pitching. You are not as good at

it as you believe you are. Let the customer draw their own conclusions. They are much better at it than you think.

- Your job is not so much to change minds it is to find open minds. The former is a lot harder than the latter, and not nearly as pragmatic. Yet sales people love the black art of selling. It really gives them a charge to feel in charge. That is why they choose the former over the latter.

- Sales people do not want to find the truth because they believe they can create the truth. Just a fancy way of saying the aforementioned.

- You cannot be part of the solution until you are part of the problem. It is very difficult to consistently show customers what is right (solution) before you show them what is wrong. If they do not trust your analysis of their problem it is very likely they will not trust your resolution.

- You do not know what you are selling until you know what the customer is avoiding, or trying to correct. Remember, customers will run 10 times as fast to avoid a problem than they will to take advantage of an opportunity.

- When you go on a sales call full of information and enthusiasm you will often go home empty-handed. It is not about you.

- You should be only as committed and enthusiastic to sell someone as they are as enthusiastic and committed to fix a problem.

- Customers buy for their reasons not ours. According to the Brooks Group the number one reason customers buy from one sales person versus another is the sales person who they choose really "got them."

- Customers love to buy, but they hate to be sold. The problem is sales people love to sell more than they love to have customers independently buy and come to their own conclusions.

- The sales person with the superior understanding of the customer's business, situation, circumstances, priorities, and problems will consistently outsell the sales person with the best product, the best price, the newest innovations, and the best offering. If sales people bought into this concept, the whole dynamics of their sale strategy would be turned upside down.

More products are bought than they are sold. More sales people are interested in winning the equivalent of the tallest midget award (selling their superior features and benefits), than just taking the time to let customers hash out the pros and cons themselves through the quality of your superior questions.

• Selling is just as much about buying as it is about selling. You also need to be sold. You need to buy into the customer's reasons for buying. Selling is a skill set of sifting, sorting and selecting opportunities so that you can carefully choose the highest prospects. Selling is a process of elimination when done properly. Selling is a process of carefully deciding who qualifies to do business with you.

42

The Change-Agent: An Impartial Facilitator

A change-agent is a sales person who takes the position that they have nothing to sell, nothing to promote until they have a thorough understanding of why a customer would want to change, buy or do anything differently.

A change-agent takes the refreshing preliminary position that they don't know what is best for their potential customer. To be an effective change-agent, be open to everything and don't have a fixed attachment to anything. That includes results and outcomes.

So selling is less about hammering home your selling points and more about peeling away the layers to promote change. Change is made easier when the salesperson lets the customer self-initiate the process by treating the customer with the power to create their own change at a comfortable pace for them.

So give your customer the personal responsibility to manage the change process, which by the way, takes the pressure off both parties at the selling event, and makes the process more open and transparent. Change truly happens more easily when it is self-directed by your customer.

From the perspective of change, things happen because other things happen. Nothing happens in a vacuum in a business. Nothing is separate, isolated or not connected. The change-agent looks always at the big picture and helps the customer see the consequences of action and inaction in a non-biased manner.

As you become an accomplished change-agent you will notice your customers so often want one result, and at the same time another part of them wants an entirely and sometimes conflicting result. Your challenge is to help put all their issues on the table and help them reconcile all their disparate goals and outcomes.

Be aware that it is difficult for customers to solve a problem on the level they perceive it. That is why the change-agent plays the role as an impartial facilitator and helps customers self-examine their issues from a different perspective and at a different level. Always let customers see the causes and the barriers before they take action to change.

An objective change-agent is always trying to enhance their value by asking themselves would the customer have paid a consulting fee for my last sales call? Would they receive enough value from my participation and insight that they would have paid a premium for my unbiased advice?

43

Too Much is Told, Too Little is Heard, Very Little Sold

We live in a time and a century of self, an image of endless explanation, for every life demands a public forum, every face a shot at fame. Traditional sales people haven't escaped this narcissistic trap. Too often sales people feel a need to project their personality or product into something that is bigger than life...an impresario.

This death march is a disturbing trend, so self-conscious and revealing, to show all and tell all about their offering, where too much is told, too little heard and not enough sold. These information sellers and product pushers thrive under the spotlight. They love the illusion of attention. They love their information cameo role. They have what I call IOD-information overload disorder. The antidote is unilateral disarmament, downsizing and decluttering of their well of information.

Customers know that conventional, information sales people are promiscuous, that they play fast and loose with their information, that they worship it as a false idol. I have personally met countless sales people who would be aghast to have sales people sell to them the way they sell to their own prospects. Because they're so self-focused they're oblivious to the impact of how they walk into sales calls overly confident of their superior firepower.

Too many sales people are working too hard to make a sale and a favorable impression. Product information is their main mantra. Surprisingly what you really have to do is simply connect with customers on a human level so they feel you understand them and get them. However, often sales people hold on to customers too tightly, while at the same time they are pushing them away.

Truth and reality of customers remain elusive to information pushers because it's all about their own truth and reality. This is why there's a big disconnect in most sales calls. When you watch closely you'll see that many customers want one thing and at the same time another part of them wants the exact opposite. This is because of lack of trust and commitment. They want insight and direction when they trust you. However, they settle for senseless information that sales people are more than happy to provide them when they don't trust that the sales person has much depth to offer.

In May 2011 The Wall Street Journal reported that big pharmaceutical companies had found replacements for the army of sales representatives that they laid off in recent years. Digital sales tools replaced human contact to tell customers vital information without the intrusion and inconvenience of having to see a sales person no matter how attractive they are. At least 25% of physician groups have today a no visit policy for sales people. Companies found that the high cost of face-to-face sales calls were being highly marginalized in this environment. They found iPad apps and a greater web presence to be equally effective and far more efficient. Obviously some sales roles are obsolete because of the perceived lack of value sales people bring to the table. Make sure yours isn't.

In the information economy you've got to provide more extra value than information regurgitation to discourage customers from cutting you out of the buying process and just clicking three times on their keyboard to get more balanced information from the web.

Sales is an input business not an output business. The more information you give out the more risk you are at getting less in return. The longer it takes to get information the more risk you are to getting information after-the-fact and when it's too late.

Take your foot off the gas when it comes to giving out information, and put the metal to the pedal when it comes to asking questions. Most sales people have false pride in regard to their expertise and product information. This just adds insult to injury and puts fuel on the fire to sell and push harder, resulting in customers and prospects pushing back, delaying and discounting what they have heard.

44

Traditional Sales Person; Someone Who Brings Confusion to Simplicity

The Rockwellian days of sales people riding high with reams of information and enthusiasm is waning dramatically. Information selling falls short of today's new generation of decision-makers who are more independent and self-initiated when it comes to educating themselves on choices and alternatives. The Internet has made the information delivery role almost entirely obsolete for sales people. Where strategic sales people create value is to help customers better understand the "tyranny of choice" – too much information. Giving more information (sell and tell) is a valueless selling proposition in most cases today.

Conventional sellers suffer from information ignorance and arrogance; too much of their own information, and not enough of the customer's information. The more information that is created for customers, the less attention they give to sellers, and the harder it is for a sales person to get the prospect's attention. Where you overuse information does not matter, until it does. And today it matters more than ever because the fiercest competitor for information for sales people is Google!

Sellers are fighting against the new normal – the Internet. Conventional sales people have lost their bearings, compass, and their reason for being in this new environment, and it is forcing a lot of them to just survive on the margins. Sales people in some cases are competing directly with their own website for being a resource for information. Customers will do as much research as they can to avoid direct contact with human beings today. As it turns out few like to talk to product mercenaries.

Many prospects will go to extremes to depersonalize and dehumanize the buying process to be spared an equally depersonalized sales pitch. In order for the customer experience to be positive, information should be used primarily as a tool for self-discovery, instead of a tool for persuasion and influence. And inexhaustible amount of information is causing customer exhaustion and indifference. It is comparable to watching paint dry. Conventional sales people over exercise their First Amendment right of freedom of speech. What they do not realize is their freedom of expression is curtailing their customer's freedom of expression. Their messaging is drowning out the customer's critical voice.

Information sellers are often problem deniers and revisionists. They try to rewrite the customer's priorities and goals to favor their solution. They disregard the disruption of change, the cost of change, and the timing of change, hoping it will be positively glossed over in the light of such an exciting future solution and positive transformation. Alas, at the same time time, customers come to their senses and deals come to a screeching halt when reality hits them squarely in the head.

Information sellers have a missionary zeal. They sell as if they have a moral product imperative to change the lives of their customers for the better. Do not get me wrong this is a noble outlook, but with foolish impracticalities. Only a sliver of the sales population can sell this way. Practical selling is simply a matching up of viable opportunities with realistic outcomes. You will not be able to be a pragmatic seller if you are ruled by a zeal of "payday emotions."

Information sellers have been taught to create value and always be telling customers something they do not know. Since the prospect does not know presumably a lot about the sales person's offering, it is automatically assumed that their target rich material of product data is just what the prospect ordered.

But what customers are really saying is tell me something I do not know about what I really care about. What they care about is whether your industry experience can translate well to helping them gain new insight into their challenges. They want your customer experience, instead of your boring solution experience. They need help in identifying and assessing, more than they need help in problem resolution. They want to feel confident that you really "get them." They need assistance in the fundamental areas of allowing them to see beyond what they see every day, but do not really.

45

When the WHY is Important Enough the What (Solution) is Secondary

To varying degrees all sales people represent risk and fear to customers; the inconvenience and burden of change. A lot of customers initially will send positive signals of interest, and then reality sets in that they will have to not only make changes with the proposed solution, but above and beyond that they will have to make difficult changes that will be felt elsewhere in the organization.

No matter how beneficial your solution is, it is an intrusion. How you manage outwardly these change considerations will greatly determine your fate. Conventional sales people throw caution to the wind and leave it to fate, and hope customers internally navigate the process, connecting all the dots, reconciling the pros and cons of change, reprioritizing their initiatives and managing conflicting office politics. This is very risky business to leave all in the hands of customers.

The change-agent, being non-partisan and unemotionally tied to outcomes, has no problem taking customers through this minefield in their pursuit of the truth and what best serves their customers.

Change-centered sales people rigorously throw away assumptions of what customers want and how they can help. They know all too well the danger and the potential that no good deed goes unpunished when they are too proactive in a dubious attempt to provide unsolicited or unwelcomed advice and solutions.

From the change-agent's perspective all action is positive. Because they are outcome neutral, all action represents progress. Good news represents a sale. Bad news early represents a lost opportunity where time, resources and effort were at a manageable level.

The change-agent is willing to examine every angle, leave no stones unturned, examine all possible options because they are not burdened like traditional sales people who have lots of conflicts of interest or contradictory motives. The down strokes are more than compensated by increasing flow of confidential information, trust, respect and deep insight.

Because a change-agent is first and foremost a business person and advisor, they do not fear hearing the truth. They give customers a wide berth to autonomously draw their own conclusions and find their own answers. They empower customers and respect their independence to make good decisions because they truly have the inside track on their own priorities.

The change-agent deals primarily in perceptions, because for customers perception is reality. To deal with customers with an even hand you have to be grounded, composed, and genuinely curious.

Orthodox sales people have a very limited grasp of reality. The only reality they focus on is their ability to provide a superior solution. Unfortunately, this is at the detriment of understanding the customer's unique reality of the cost of change. Because of this sales people do not represent critical thinking and certainly are not viewed as the voice of reason.

Customers and traditional sales people live in their own realities. Neither is willing to bridge the gap. That is why there is lots of mistrust, misinformation and limited flow of important information.

46

You Will Get Truthful Answers When You Start Giving Truthful Questions

A non-selling posture tries to see everything with an open and expansive mind and without personal and product identification. It neither attacks or defends. Attacking and defending ends up being the same thing; a weakness. Attacking your competition or vigorously defending your offering only marginalizes your selling position. The only time to justify your authority is when you attack your customer's problems by getting to the root causes and helping them assess the cost of changing.

The non-selling posture is all about being centered and grounded. There are no wide extremes of blue skying your product attributes, or wildly defending against objections and resistance, because you cannot be in the right, or be right, while at the same time repudiating what is wrong, or opposing others who are wrong and misinformed.

When one is centered one ends up accepting their customers for who they are and honoring them for whatever position they may be in. Do not think you know what ultimately is best for them. You never will. There are too many variables and unknowns that you will never have access to. When you stop imposing your will on your customers, you stop complaining and taking it personally when they do not heed your advice. This is very refreshing for most sales people who find many elements of selling to be manipulative, overly aggressive, frustrating and even cheesy.

Do not confuse a non-selling posture with being passive, apathetic, inactive and nonchalant. The non-selling posture is a powerful tool that gets customers to exchange sensitive and important information because the sales person is nonthreatening, disarming, balanced in their approach and authentic in their desire to uncover the truth.

A strategic sales person is like a forensic tax investigator. They do not take anything at face value, they sniff around for clues and evidence, they are always looking for patterns of behavior, looking for true motives and looking for contradictory statements and evidence.

The reality is customers will give you more truthful answers if you give them more truthful questions; questions that are fair-minded and unbiased. You will also get to the truth quicker when you temper your enthusiasm. "Enthusiasm is contagious" is an old and archaic sales tenet. Today, enthusiasm is contagious, and it is a killer. Enthusiastic selling's fatal flaw is a loss of objectivity and credibility. It is very difficult to be enthusiastic and at the same time explore and expose serious problems. It is totally out of context. Enthusiastic selling has a very limited place in the information economy where customers are not looking for enthusiastic packaging of product information, but are looking more for insight and understanding.

A strategic sales person is like a forensic tax investigator. They do not take anything at face value, they sniff around for clues and evidence, they are always looking for patterns of behavior, looking for true motives and looking for contradictory statements and evidence.

The reality is customers will give you more truthful answers if you give them more truthful questions; questions that are fair-minded and unbiased. You will also get to the truth quicker when you temper your enthusiasm. "Enthusiasm is contagious" is an old and archaic sales tenet. Today, enthusiasm is contagious, and it is a killer. Enthusiastic selling's fatal flaw is a loss of objectivity and credibility. It is very difficult to be enthusiastic and at the same time explore and expose serious problems. It is totally out of context. Enthusiastic selling has a very limited place in the information economy where customers are not looking for enthusiastic packaging of product information, but are looking more for insight and understanding.

Ask questions that customers are afraid to ask of themselves. Questions that appear to weaken the sales person's position or negotiating posture generally will be viewed as risk-free on the part of the customer and therefore they are more likely to answer it truthfully.

Control and power over customers are weaknesses disguised as strengths. A non-selling posture is achieved when one refuses all forms of external authority and control. One's selling position becomes more tenuous when one wants credit, control, ownership and validation. Keep in mind to remain in charge of a sales call, you need to give up being in charge.